A Marshmallow on the Bus:
A Collection of Stories
Written on the MTA

by

ANNE BORN

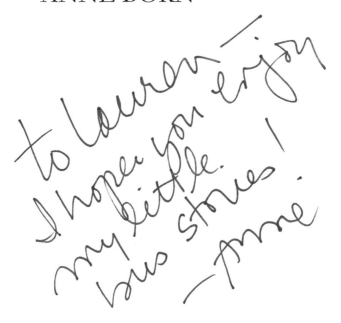

to lauren!
I hope you enjoy
my little
bus stories!
— anne

Dedication

*To Lucy, Charlie, Mary Dorothy, Graceanna;
to their dad and to my dad. You are all
smart, beautiful, and important.*

Table of Contents

Acknowledgments

These stories began their public lives as blog posts on both *Open Salon*, where I am known as Nilesite, and *Red Room*, where I am known as Anne Born. I started writing them in 2010, but it was only when we moved to the Bronx that I was given the opportunity to spend some serious time on them. I moved from a one-bus commute to work to a two-bus commute and because neither bus ride was long enough for me to get anything out of my book club book, I stared out the window. I'd see things I would want to describe to my children when I got home but I kept forgetting the details. That's when I decided to start making notes which became stories or poems.

Eventually, I quit the book club and kept writing. Sometimes I would add photographs, if I saw something fun or unusual, but most times, I would just tell the story. So, I would like to thank first the MTA for giving me a comfy place to work for these past years and my friends and family who have had to put up with me while the stories developed.

This collection would never have taken shape without the support of my colleagues at Columbia University where I worked for 13 years; including, but certainly not limited to George, Stacey, Lourdes, Patrick, Millie, Bill, Deb C., Deb M., Dina, Sally, Marlene, Lalla, Joy, JoAnn, Pam R., Micaela, Kay, Lani, Angela, Ruby, Hazel, Sheridan, Bob and Kerry, Jan and Bidi, Robert H., Dan R., and Dora. I am, as my mother would have said, proud to know you.

I would like to single out Emily Gabor for being the very first person to read and share one of my early *Open Salon* stories about churches.

I would also like to give a grateful nod to my two Bronx bus buddies: Betty and Aubrey. They put up with me talking through the stories and sharing my photos. Anyone who is willing to look at your vacation photos is a special friend.

And it's important to recognize the members of your family who support the crazy things you do: my dad and my cousins Joann, Jim, Debbie, Kevin, Larry, Maria, Bill, Marian, and their kids. And, of course, Mike and The Babies.

I have a number of wonderful imaginary friends who also deserve mention here – they have nudged me, prompted me, praised me, and critiqued me and my writing for the past three years. Unlike the friends I see, these are friends, for the most part, who I have never met. We write together every day, in different cities, in different states, in several different countries, and we come together online to share what bothers us, what inspires us, and what really upsets us, and remarkably, even though we may not share a real geographic location, we share quite a bit of life. This is for you Jane, Huntington, Mary, Katherine, Loren, Barbara, Rosy, Judee; Lea, Gerald, Alysa, skypixio, tink, 'bug, Joan, Jeanne, Richard, Jonathan, Con, Kim, P Dubs, Phyllis, Kate, Andy, Zanelle, Nikki, Bernadine, Linda, M.C.S., John, Libby, Sally, Gabby, jmac, Candace, Anne, Jaime, Emily C., kosher, Susan, Ande, Daniel R., designanator, L.C.; Joanne, Aliza, Lisa, Tina, and so many more talented writers – you are only imaginary to everyone else. To me, you are quite real and quite wonderful.

They say there are eight million stories in the naked city. If you've got a minute, I'd like to tell them to you.

Introduction

When you think of writers working on their stories, the great novels, the insightful poems, you probably think, like I used to, that the best work gets done in calm seclusion. There's a fire crackling in the fireplace, a soft snowfall outside the frost-tinged windows. Or the writer has a huge open desk, piled high with research and inspiration, a broad view of the ocean in the direct line of sight from the Widow's Walk of a greying Victorian manse.

Well, neither works for me. When I was in college, I used to go to the local fried chicken place instead of the library. I knew too many people at the library and the French fries kept me going. And now, I write on the bus or the subway. If I have that much time to myself – meaning I don't know anybody in the bus or on that train car – then I am grateful and I am writing.

Sometimes, I write *about* the bus, as in *Next Bus Please* or *The Limited Lament* and other days, I am completely captivated with some random event taking place near my bus stop, as in *The Hippy on Primary Day* or *Selling Usage to a Writer Waiting for The Bus*. There are days when the view out the window is something that just doesn't leave until I make sense of it on paper, like *The Life of a Squirrel*.

I've never considered myself a poet even though a local bar has designated me, along with everyone who reads there in their once-a-month open mics, a "local poet." But what I have learned is that the genre will present itself. *The River* was prompted by a dear friend named Kate. She surfaces in *Days, Dates, and Places. Daybreak* came to me when I hopped off my bus and found myself in Riverside Park watching a homeless woman gather up her plastic bags. I felt helpless – I realized if I gave her all I had with me at that moment, it would not change her life significantly. She would go through the cash in a day and my jacket and shoes in a few weeks, given that she was sleeping outdoors.

But it was when I started writing *Watching* that I felt I could call myself a poet. I knew I could never express that terrible anguish any other way.

Part of the reason I find the MTA in New York so compelling is that I grew up with cars, not daily rides on public transportation. In many ways, getting on the train in the morning is like riding an amusement ride at a theme park. The theme is not always clear to me, but the riders are so interesting and the stations are all different.

You could try to characterize how the stations and bus shelters represent their neighborhood, but you'd probably be wrong. There's the violinist on the platform on the Upper West Side in the morning or the guy with the misspelled sign on his coffee cart – but both of them had to travel at least some distance to get there. It's a function of a process in flux – everyone moves, nothing sticks in place. Some days, I feel like a huge carousel has slowed down just long enough for me to swing up and grab a horse.

I feel that it's necessary to mention that although I have lived in New York for 35 years, I am no expert. I get flummoxed giving tourists direction and just a few weeks ago, I sent a lovely Asian couple in the wrong direction when they asked how to get to Rockefeller Center. It's hopeless – the city is too big, too distracting. I have never been to Staten Island, or the Top of the Rock. I've never seen the end of the New York Marathon, and I have never walked across the Brooklyn Bridge. But I have lived in three wonderful neighborhoods and, every day, I am getting to know my way around this city one bitty bit better at a time.

The bus riding continues. The writing continues.

Rule one of reading other people's stories is that whenever you say 'well that's not convincing' the author tells you that's the bit that wasn't made up. This is because real life is under no obligation to be convincing.

—Neil Gaiman

How could
I not have
chosen this
before?

Sketch by Ellen Stedfeld, May 21, 2014, Inspired Word at
Coffeed, Long Island City, New York

Next Bus Please

It was a tiny bit warmer this morning, but still not comfortable if you are standing on a street corner, waiting for the bus. It's the one real deal breaker. It can be warm enough walking, or warm enough on a subway platform, but there are corners in Manhattan in particular that defy even the most stalwart of bus riders. And the worst part of it? When the bus you see in the distance says, "Next Bus Please."

I had coffee with me this morning, so I was braced. The bus pulled up to the stoplight and I looked up at the driver who opened the door and waved at me to come, get on his bus. The sign was still a foreboding "Next Bus Please," but I thought, how scary is this really when all the buses stopping at this corner go to my stop anyway?

I stepped up and asked the driver, "So, where are we going today?" The driver boasted, "All the way to South Ferry, ma'am." I paid my fare and took my seat. And I was the only one on a completely empty bus. In rush hour.

In that flash of a moment, in that pinprick of a second, I thought to myself, "The possibilities are endless." I have an entire New York City bus to myself and a driver who is not advertising our route – even though I knew it had to be the M5 bus. That's the one that goes from that corner to South Ferry.

What if we were to go all the way to South Ferry together, him and me, without picking up any more riders? That would be so cool! Just to be honest, I have to say I'm not really sure where South Ferry is exactly – I'm fairly certain it's where you get the Staten Island Ferry which I have never taken. I am sure there's no North Ferry.

What if I decided in that brilliant moment not to get off at my stop? Would I change the course of history like Captain Kirk and Mr. Spock when they went back to pre-WWII on *Star Trek*?

A Marshmallow on the Bus

Would the driver talk to me? I'd talk to him. Should I be coy and reticent or bold and adventurous? I could be sassy and let him know I really knew his route. Or I could just fold up on myself and play Angry Birds on my iPhone.

I wondered how long it would take for him to forget I was there. He would just keep driving this mystery bus with only one invisible passenger until we got to South Ferry where I could bid him a saucy goodbye.

But, by the time we reached the next limited bus stop at 145th Street, he'd turned on the M5 sign, replacing the "Next Bus Please." A woman with a fleecy black hat, a girl with hot pink gloves and a rhinestone iPhone cover, and a guy with Beats headphones got on and took their seats.

Ten minutes later, I got off at the library. The course of history was left unchanged.

Waiting with the Spuds

I take lots of buses in New York. I have always preferred buses to trains and I try to make sure I have a notebook or a few sale catalogs to read while I go from Point A to Point B. Buses have come a long way since I moved here many years ago, no pun intended. They are heated and cooled as the weather demands, the drivers are about 78% friendly on any given day, and for the most part, buses are fairly quiet. But I always keep my iPod in my bag to drown out the occasional noisy iPod or cellphone conversation of my fellow passengers.

Along with more comfortable buses, we have more comfortable bus shelters and that's where I spotted the spuds. I was walking down Broadway and saw two white plastic I "heart" NY bags on the bench at the bus stop on 116th Street. Well, the NYPD keeps reminding us that if we see something, we should say something, so I took a closer look and found many eyes looking back at me. In the two plastic bags were about 18 fresh, Idaho potatoes. Then, I didn't know what I was supposed to say.

"911 Operator, what's your emergency?"

"Yes, ma'am, I'm on Broadway in front of Ollie's and I see something. There's these two bags of potatoes sitting here, waiting for the bus."

Click.

A car pulled up to see what I was looking at and then drove off. It would not have been good to start a gaper's block over Idaho potatoes. And a couple of people walked by, looked in, kept moving. So I took a couple of photos with my phone and walked on. But I couldn't help wondering the fate of the taters. They blocked one third of the bench so only two people could sit comfortably next to them assuming you *could* sit comfortably next to two bags of potatoes. They didn't seem to belong to anyone, so I guess they would be sitting there for a while. I can't imagine someone picking up the two bags and walking away with them because that's kind of icky. In New York, we tend to shun food that is left sitting on a bus bench, for so many reasons.

So wither the praties? It'd be nice if they got wherever they were going, but I kind of doubt it, knowing what I know about potatoes and bus shelters. Still, there was a wonderfully whimsical quality to our encounter, like they all looked up for just that moment and wondered if I'd take them home and give them a hot bath and a mash.

My guess is that some random sanitation worker or bus shelter maintenance guy tossed them. It's sad not to get where you wanted to go.

Urban Bus Anthropology

Sometimes I read on the bus, sometimes I look out the window, but lately, I have been surveying the floor and I feel like someone who has stumbled across a lost civilization, hoping against hope that there is enough left among their shards, clay pipes, and buttons to give a clear picture of the folks who lived there.

This is complicated, of course, for many reasons, not the least of which is that city buses are cleaned all the time. You'd never know it if you are on the back end of the day's run, but I get on my first bus early in the day when the seats are still damp from the sprays of the night before.

But even then, you can see traces of the passengers who were there just before you. They drop mittens, although rarely both. They drop barely read newspapers, but rarely magazines. Does this say that two mittens have more value than one? Or that magazines that you pay for have more value than the free newspapers with all the ads? I'm not sure.

In the case of the mittens, the sad soul who dropped just one, now lives with the diminished value of the other, but the newspaper reader's commute is improved by not having to lug around that weighty tome or be embarrassed by the fact he was reading a freebie instead of the costly *Wall Street Journal* or *New York Times*. You pretty much never see anyone leaving those behind. It's probably that their ensemble, their look is only complete by carrying an expensive paper that shouts, "I can read!"

The MTA in New York has a lost and found office that sounds really efficient when you read their FAQs. If you leave something with your name and phone number or address on it, they will contact you. So much for the mitten owners. And if you are quick about it, you can circumvent the inevitable by tracking down the exact bus that you were on so your lost item can be returned to you before it gets to their center. I imagine it looks like that last scene in the *Indiana Jones* movie, with miles of cardboard boxes of indeterminate provenance with rampant mislabeling. They say they will keep your mitten for a few months before it's auctioned off to the highest bidder, although I can't imagine anyone attending such a sad event in the hopes of reuniting one mitten with the other. After that, the leftover stuff is destroyed.

The rest of the bits and pieces left on the bus floor tell me that the MTA should provide used gum receptacles and some place to put our empty fast food drink cups. Sometimes you see MetroCards looking up at you from under a seat. I think these probably don't have any fares left on them, but you never know. I once picked up a cashmere Burberry scarf that was left on the floor in the back of the bus. I took it to the cleaners, knowing its retail value, but I only wore it a few times before leaving it on another bus for someone else to find. It was less about paying it forward and more about how I never really could make it mine.

Sometimes you see used Kleenexes from somebody with something scary contagious. Sometimes there are torn up bits of lists that someone left behind, and sometimes there are the random pieces of change, a nickel or a dime usually dropped on the way to the fare box. It's bad form to stop and pick that up. It just seems wrong somehow. And it only says that even though everyone complains that the fares are high, someone had change left over after paying their fare. They just didn't know they'd left it on the bus.

Looking at the floor is fast becoming my favorite bus thing to do. After all, if you take the same route every day, the chance of something changing outside the window is slim. But the chance to experience the flow of humanity grows every time I get on the bus.

Selling 'Usage to a Writer Waiting for the Bus

So, there's this coffee cart. When I am waiting for the bus, I stand on the sidewalk and face this cart from across the street. It's directly across the street from my first bus stop in the morning, in my direct line of sight. Unavoidable. The cart is covered with both print and neon advertising and it's hugely misspelled.

The little neon crawl that advertises the cart's wares zips along, blinking madly, flashing the menu. It is silent, but compelling. Every single day, I am forced to read along. I can try looking away, but since I have waited for the bus here every morning for the past three and a half years already, I know I'm going to be reading it, over and over again, like there's some invisible yet insistent, crazy, cosmic energy dragging me to it.

It starts with "You welcome to" and the suspense just builds from there. Where am I welcome? What happened to the verb, you "are" welcome?

OK, I'm game, what's next? These crazy – yet innocuous – blinking, geometric, flashing words: "Steve's Place." Ah, I am welcome to Steve's Place.

Then the sign starts to degrade. We have already sacrificed the "are," but now? In the next screen shot, Steve becomes "Steuve." You (are) welcome to Steuve's Place.

I think the yellow and green lights just needed another character, another letter, so Steve became "Steuve" to eat up the extra digital space. Either that, or Steve is not the correct spelling and Steuve is the real name of the coffee guy.

And so it goes. There's "baels and hot chocolate" instead of "bagels and hot chocolate" and "usage with coffe" instead of "sausage with coffee." It all blinks and flashes along and it's looped so it will go on for eternity.

Two things: there's this interesting thing I learned from a Spanish professor at Columbia University who studies medieval manuscript marginalia. He says everyone reads the marginalia along with the text on the page because, by nature, you are forced to read anything in front of you. That's why everyone reads the cereal box again and again when it sits on the breakfast table while you eat the Wheaties. It's why you read every T-shirt that walks by and the headlines on newspapers at magazine stands. And it's why I stand there, robotically reading along with this neon crawl until my bus arrives and I am released.

The other thing is more troubling: how can Steve not know his sign is completely corrupted? Did he buy a pig in a poke? Did the sign seller install it and run? Or does Steve really just set up the cart and start selling "coffe" without the slightest notion that the sign is hopelessly off?

It's a conundrum. One that faces me every day. I have resisted asking Steve if he knows, but the longer this goes on, the more I feel equally compelled to try the "coffe."

Maybe with a "bael."

Or some usage.

Trains in Tandem

When you grow up in the Midwest, you get used to the sound of trains. American trains crisscross America's heartland accompanied by lowered gates, blinking lights, whistles, and bells. But most of the trains I remember were not passenger trains. They carried freight from here to there and back. We'd take passenger trains once in a while in and out of Chicago, but for the most part, the train experience for me was more observation than participation.

That all changed when I moved to New York. Even though we do have our fair share of freight trains passing through, it's the subway that fascinates me. I get to ride trains any time I want and, even after all these years, there are a couple of things that I really enjoy.

I love to watch two trains come into the station at the same time. You stand on the platform at these random moments, and both the local and the express come speeding in, one on either side of you, until there's nothing but train cars left and right.

Yesterday, I got on a regular local train in my neighborhood, heading downtown. There was a "sleepy guy" sitting opposite me as I took my seat. It was unremarkable to see passengers asleep on the train in the early morning but I noticed him because his black sneakers were trimmed in blazing white. You don't see that all that often. He snoozed, I watched, and the train made its way downtown, making one stop before coming into the first express stop. We pulled in at the same time as an express train on the adjacent track and I jumped off my local to get on it.

And so did the sleepy guy, apparently, because when I sat down and looked up to survey my new surroundings, he was suddenly sitting across from me again, and asleep again. I shrugged and started looking out the windows.

That's when I noticed the local train. Running immediately alongside my new express train was the train I had just left. For just a few seconds, we were traveling in awkward proximity to the exact car I had just left along with all the local riders I had just left. Here I was with the sleepy guy and there were all the other folks on the local; me watching them as they were watching us. We, the ones who betrayed them, the ones who thought we were better than them. And then they were gone as we sped past to the next express stop and their train slowed to pull into their local stop.

When I got off at my stop, the sleepy guy got off with me and then he disappeared into the street. It was a moment of serendipity.

A Marshmallow on the Bus

If you live in a big city like New York full time and don't come and go as a visitor or a guest, I think you tend to take some very random things for granted. You know the bus schedules are more guidelines than anything resembling a schedule, you know that people pretty much never step aside to let you on or off the trains, you know that no cab drivers know how to get to Yankee Stadium from anywhere, and you know that when spring comes, it's always as if you never saw it before. I have been trying lately not to take so much for granted and it has given me a new appreciation for this amazing town.

New York is rarely as beautiful as Woody Allen would have you believe, but it can be pretty quirky in a way that I have not experienced outside the five boroughs. For me, it's all in the stuff that you just step over on your way from here to there. You've got the grey-green, drizzly schmutz that pools on the sidewalk after the trash is collected. And the wrappers and cups from folks who missed the memo about cleaning up after themselves, and there's the random sock or glove that is left when its mate decides to move on without it.

This morning, there was a marshmallow on the bus.

I rode this particular bus for 15 minutes this morning, all the while just opposite a single marshmallow that was sitting alone on the sticky, icky floor. A couple of things struck me. First, I wanted to know how one, lone marshmallow got on the bus in the first place. Did it come with all its fresh little buddies, all tightly plastic-wrapped in their bag? If that's the case, how did this one little guy slip out? Was it somebody's idea of a healthy snack and it got on in a Ziploc with other marshmallows? Probably not, because I am the only person I know who snacks on marshmallows and, more importantly, I left all my marshmallows at home.

Maybe some kid was bartering his lunch for hers and the marshmallow was left behind in the bargain. This is hard to believe though. How could you deliberately drop a marshmallow on the floor of the bus? That's just wrong.

Maybe this was the odd marshmallow out? There were the two lunch swappers and there were five marshmallows in the Ziploc so two went to him, two went to her, and one was deposited on the bus? It's not the best way to pay it forward because the bus floor can be a dark and foreboding place, all in all, and the life expectancy of the marshmallow is shorter there than just about anywhere else.

I realize I could have swished it out the door with my foot when I got off at my stop, but I was so fascinated watching it sit there in all its fluffy white perfection. At least a dozen people walked over it to get on and off the bus, maybe more, depending on when it landed on the floor. What I do know is that it is going to meet one of two outcomes and probably has already, given that this happened hours ago. Either everyone who gets on and off the bus will respect the sovereignty of the marshmallow and keep stepping over it, or it will get squished. You can see right away why you'd want to step *over* rather than step on a single marshmallow. Squish is not good for either of you.

So this is my ode to a single, bus-riding marshmallow. I do not know where you came from or where you went on the bus after I got off on Broadway this morning. But you were part of the greater wonder of New York today and I salute you.

Hanging Moon

I caught sight of a morning moon,
hanging low in a clear
   sky blue sky.

I saw it over the bail bonds office
   and that real estate place that's never open.
I look up at the planes
taking the sky from you
   as you watch back at
the newspaper guy
catching up with his friends
supplicants on their way to the courts
and the buses
   inching their way to the City.

You are not moving, moon.

But, when I come home,
   you are the only thing in all this space
that will be gone.
Nothing, nothing changes here 'cept you.

I will look for you
again in the morning.
Behind the buildings,
across the street,
up the block,
over the bail bonds office
and that real estate place that's never open.

Hanging shy.

Sitting in One of My Father's Many Mansions

Subway train cars during rush hour in New York are claustrophobia-inducing. You stand on the platform, waiting for the train with a thousand strangers and then you're off, standing on the train – in the midst of a thousand strangers. Typically, this is why you are admonished not to make eye contact. You really don't want to bother strangers during rush hour.

Well, that might be typical, but not this week. This week, two working evangelists found enough space to ply their trade and market their wares and it all took place on the D train between Yankee Stadium in the Bronx and Rockefeller Center in Manhattan.

On Wednesday, I got on the train and found myself about six feet away from a shouter. Shouters, as I call them, are the Bible-waving, gay-fearing folks who consume most of the air in the train by shouting out that we, the listeners, are all likely to go to Hell if we don't pay attention to what they have to say. In this case, it was an African woman with a thick French accent who was waving the book at us and shouting, "Jesus loves you Jesus loves you Jesus loves you!"

Shouters usually work in train cars that are full, but not packed. They walk up and down in the center of the train car and they have a stage for their message. It's like watching a well-rehearsed one-man or one-woman show. They don't ask for money – they just want your soul. So, you can see why this act might play out differently if the train is wall-to-wall, jam-packed as it is at rush hour.

But that did not deter this woman. She continued her mission in both French and English, at the top of her lungs, in the car completely filled with people. She was just out of sight but certainly not out of earshot and, from what I could determine, people ignored her as if she were one of the cardboard signs advertising the way to clear skin rather than the path to salvation. Loud, intrusive, insistent, and largely ignored, she got off at 125th Street where I saw the most remarkable bit of her story. She was accompanied by two small children with backpacks and lunch boxes who looked like they were on their way to school. She had disciples.

On Thursday, I sat next to a man who was the opposite of a shouter. He was a friendly guy. Friendly guys are the evangelists who sit next to you and start innocent conversations that almost always end up with something about God creating Adam and Eve and not Adam and *Steve*. Unlike the shouters, it's actually the friendly guys who are more like stand-up comedians. They want to relate, they want to become your friend, and they weave their stories endlessly. This particular friendly guy spoke to two people sitting next to him for the entire 30 minutes it took to get from my stop to their stop. When they got off, he wished them a blessed day and started right in on the unsuspecting woman who took their seats when they left.

The friendly guy had the approach of, "Am I right, or am I right?" He looked for affirmation of his every sentence from his two captives. He told them about mapping the human genome and how that proved he was not a horse. "So don't come out of the closet and suddenly say you're a horse – I am so disgusted by that." And he told them that both his wife and his son were poisoned by toxic fruit and that's why he buys only organic produce because "They" are trying to poison us.

The shouter was happy, confident, assured of her place in Heaven among the blessed. The friendly guy: fearful, apprehensive, suspicious, disgusted. Yet both of them were trying to make us follow them – they both wanted, in that crowded space, to sway us all to their way of thinking, one by one, or many at one blow. I'm not sure why either of them thought this was their best venue – most other performers, singers or comedians, pick their club carefully to get the best crowd for their material. It could be that they have made a pact with God to present what they believe is His message at every opportunity and this crowded rush hour train was just that. Or it could be that they were so caught up in their mission that they didn't even notice that they were surrounded by a thousand strangers. To them, it could be they were surrounded by a thousand potential converts.

In the end, all I could think of was the scene in the Gospel of John where Jesus says His father's house has many mansions (John 14:2). This week, the downtown express D train was one of them.

The John 14:6 Guy in Harlem

There is this guy. I watched him the other day. He was leaning into the passenger side of a decorated car parked on Broadway where there was a pile of white papers and some Scotch tape on the front seat. Then he stood next to the open door and looked around, like he was looking for someone. That's how he caught my eye.

A moment later, turning back to the car, he pulled out a single sheet of paper and, leaning against the car, he carefully stretched tape across the top and bottom of the paper, sticky side down. He left the passenger door open, walked about 20 feet up the street, and slapped the paper on the bus shelter, next to a vodka ad. It said, on five lines of all-cap type, "JESUS I AM THE WAY THE TRUTH THE LIFE JOHN 14:6."

This was the John 14:6 Guy.

Copies of this 8.5" x 11" John 14:6 sign are plastered over dozens of previously blank spots on walls and telephone poles and hydrants all over Manhattan and the Bronx. They are so much a regular part of the daily landscape that I don't even notice them much anymore, but now I know where they come from. What I do not know however, is what difference they make.

This verse is popular enough. It surfaces in hymns and sermons. It's a verse most people have heard in one context or the other. Jesus was asked how you get to the Kingdom of Heaven and he says that He is the way. But what are we supposed to get out of reading the verse again and again everywhere? Especially, when it's not part of a sermon, what's the point?

I think it's safe to assume that people who see this flier will fall roughly into three categories. First, we have the Already Saved who will nod and acknowledge that the verse is both familiar and comforting. Jesus, to them, *is* the way, and amen to that. Then, there are those Already Saved who understand the verse, but they just don't need to see Jesus fliers on their bus stops. The third group is seriously not all that interested. I would call them Everyone Else, or the "Please stop trying to save me" group.

This flier will accomplish its task with the Already Saved and it will be no more than a mild irritation to the "I do not want to see Bible verses on my bus stop" group. But how would you know if it made any difference to Everyone Else?

This is what fascinates me about all those lovely folks who hand out little religious pamphlets. If I wanted you to come to my church, I guess I would station myself near the building and speak to passersby about the lovely architecture, the welcoming services, the opportunity to become part of a vibrant, caring community. At least I would be able to gauge my effectiveness by being able to see if you ever showed up at the church.

But what would motivate me to print hundreds of fliers to Scotch tape on bus stops without the proximity to my church? Why adopt that scatter shot approach? It's fairly labor intensive to post these fliers and even more so if there's no way to determine the effectiveness of the activity. There's no reference in any of this literature to suggest an organization behind it, no mention of a website where you could get information about 14:6 meetings or events. There's nothing in this particular bit of evangelization that speaks of an affiliation with a church group, a specific denomination, or a preacher. And there's no mention of donations or collecting money. There was just that one guy: his tape, his fliers, his colorful car.

Taking this scenario a step further, I have to ask if maybe the direct and only benefit from this exercise of printing fliers and taping them to bus stops is to the taper, to that one guy. What if that one guy is following some kind of mission and he is inner-driven to remind people that, in his view, Jesus really is the way. It could be just that the activity is its own reward.

Once all the papers are posted, this one guy can go home and read his own Bible in the peace that comes from having done something to encourage the rest of us to do the same thing. To a lot of people, it could be just another example of the worst kind of littering, but to this one guy, it's his lot in life. He's the 14:6 Guy.

When my bus pulled up, I watched him walk across the street, under the subway tracks that cross 125th Street at Broadway. He was wearing one of his own signs on a string around his neck and a red Jesus baseball cap.

In that moment, my life seemed so very complicated and his, so simple.

Daybreak

What must daybreak be like
     when you've slept all night
     on a bench in the park,
Surrounded by the cool breeze off the river,
covered by tall trees,
     Your stolen grocery cart
in front of you, filled with all those plastic bags?

     I can't shelter you.

On my way to work, off the bus,
     wearing my clean clothes
     and my favorite shoes,
carrying breakfast from a store,
the change in my pocket.

What you need, I have.
What you want, I can't imagine.

What I have is never enough.
I already have more today,
but I will want more tomorrow.

     I don't need a thing.

A Hippy on Primary Day

It's primary day in New York and pretty much every
street corner has someone out pressing the flesh, as they
used to say, handing out fliers, hoping to get your attention
just long enough to let you know they back one candidate or
another for the political jobs that are up for grabs today. I'm
not sure what caught my eye about this one woman this
morning, but it was probably the weaving, the crisscrossing-
the-sidewalk motion she made, making sure she spoke to
everyone who came by her on their way to the train.

She was working the block where I catch my second
bus. She had long, dangling earrings and she was older, older
than me certainly, with short, cropped gray hair. Her haircut
looked like she'd cut it herself and it badly needed a trim. Her
skirt was overlong, striped canvas, hanging almost to her
ankles. She wore battered Birkenstocks with the three straps
buckled across the top of her bare feet. The lightweight,
white, V-necked blousy top had blue wild flowers
embroidered on the front and long bell bottom sleeves that
were trimmed in the same blue flowers and wider than her
wrists at the hem.

She was a hippy; an older version of her long ago self,
still handing out political news of some candidate, some issue,
something she hoped everyone else would care about as
much as she does. She had a TWU plastic shopping bag
hanging over her arm, the embodiment of a lifelong choice
for activism instead of lethargy, revolution instead of the
predictable comfort of the status quo. I'm certain she's calling
her handouts "fliers" now. In the 60s, she probably used to
call them "pamphlets" or "leaflets," words no longer in use.

I wanted to see what was in her leather messenger
bag. Does she keep things in there that no self-respecting
hippy would own? Does she have keys to a nice duplex with a
river view or an iPhone with Twitter and Facebook or the
latest games on it? Or is this someone who still lives in a tiny,
cluttered, rent-controlled studio with her cats and books,

recycling every bread wrapper, and taking her homemade yogurt with her to marches and sit-ins?

The very idea of keeping up with the politics of every generation for the past 50 years exhausts me, but here she is, handing out fliers. I wonder if she goes downtown to hand out granola bars to the Occupy Wall Street people, but more importantly, I wonder why does that bother me?

I wanted to yell, "Act your age already! The revolution never came because we never really wanted it." I felt like she needed to understand that the rest of us left school and got jobs and raised families the best way we knew how and left her to hand out the fliers. There is no doubt in my mind that my life was made better because she chose to work so hard all these years for social justice and peace.

So why do I begrudge her now the opportunity to keep doing it, to keep hoping that change is always better than what we have, and that tomorrow is only better if we make it so?

She makes me feel guilty.

I feel guilty that she is doing this and I reap the benefits without even taking one of her fliers. I live in another district so I don't even know what they were running for or why they were so important to her today, but in the end, I hope her people win. Even if she does go home to that snazzy, expensive duplex with the river views.

The People on the Bus

The people I see on the bus do not go up and down. Most days, bus people are like those slim, phosphorescent sea animals, so close to the bottom, skimming the ocean floor in total darkness, airless, with the weight of tons and gallons of water pressing down on them. Remarkably, they survive there, living out of sight, invisible to land animals. In the few videos I have seen of these sea-bed animals, they scatter from view once the light comes on them, as if they could find substantive shelter in the dark. Dark protects them.

Bus people come in varieties, categories. Early in the morning, when I am going downtown, in the light of a new day, I see the maids and housekeepers who are on their way to the Upper East Side. They wear lightweight pants with heavy sneakers and they always carry the tools of their trade: mops, cleansers, rags, paper towels. Sometimes they carry it all – everything – in flimsy, white plastic shopping bags. The more organized among them will have small-wheeled, canvas and metal carts that they can drag on and off the bus. I wonder, do they have to buy their own supplies, paying out of their own pocket for these things, or do their employers send them out to buy what they need? Sometimes, they get on with their daughters.

After the maids, come the people who sleep. It's difficult to determine where they got on or where they are going because they are not really getting anywhere. Sleepers tend to sit in the back, as if that distance from the driver protects them from being awakened and tossed off the bus. They lean against the windows and you could think they were just looking out. But these are not the regular riders. Sleepers tend only to appear once and then not again. Somehow, I doubt they ever get where they were going, and it's possible this was just a way station in a day of being homeless or lost or shut out of a family home. Or just dirt tired.

There is a woman who sits right behind the driver, and she is the first person I see when I board. She is the anomaly, a regular sleeper. She's a triangular shape, all wide at the middle and pointy at the ends. Her hair was dyed, say, eight months ago, based on the fresh growth of gray hair behind the orange. Her mouth lags open and she leans as if something I can't see pulls her down to one side. Sometimes, she rallies and looks around for a second before sinking back into what seems like a flat, dreamless sleep. I don't see her get on and she sleeps past my stop, but I have seen her many times. She carries a plastic bag.

It's more difficult to watch the children who sleep on the bus. They never time it right and are always just fully asleep when their mothers are trying to get them off the bus. They are dragged, pushed, propped up, and shouted at on the way off the bus and then berated mercilessly when they are on the street for falling asleep, as if they could have stopped themselves and did not. The mothers are angry and the children are still drowsy and confused as they trip up the street on their way to school.

The morning Bible people on the bus tend to keep to themselves and they don't spout off about getting saved like the afternoon Bible people who preach on the train. They come in two sets, divided by gender: the middle-aged ladies who read tracts and the older men who carry thick, full-sized black books. The tracts look fresh, for the most part, as if someone had just provided them with early morning prayers to read. But the Bibles are worn, dog-eared, underlined, and highlighted. One man alternates between his Bible and his book *about* the Bible. I cannot imagine how you can read the same book, regardless of its complexity or impact, every day for months, years, but they do. I wonder if they are the ones who can quote verses at the drop of a hat: like John, Chapter 13, Verse 35.

There are the angry people. It's hard to say what else binds this group together because they masquerade as single riders until the driver misses their stop. Then, all of a sudden, they mass and swarm around the oversight, rising like hungry gulls who swoop to feed on dead fish washed up on the beach. Where these people did not interact before, now they shout together, nodding in agreement, swaying in unison from side to side to make the point that lives were thrown into jeopardy because they now had to walk back to their stop. This sudden surge of anger and rage is what pulls this group together the same way pride and a love of the sport is what pulls soccer fans together. In one instant, random strangers on a shared public conveyance, going to different places, draw to a center of shared outrage.

Buses also carry drug dealers who sit in the back, methodically emptying the contents of cheap cigars to fill the skins with their product. Buses carry the lame who lift their walkers and ride alone.

But ultimately, buses are about waiting. You get on and you wait until it's time to get off. It's a suspended activity, an illusion of progress, but that's not to say nothing's happening. Some days, it's like sitting in the audience of a free theater. Other days, it's as if the whole population of riders is swept in off the street by the same ocean wave and then tossed back out again as the bus pulls up to their stop where they rush out, unaware they are dripping wet from the experience.

On the Concourse

It's still now,
Between midnight and daylight
And all I hear is the wind.

The tree across the street drags its branches
across the bricks
Empty plastic bags rustle
across the sidewalk.

And past that, there's another layer
A circle away from me
Where the sound of tires on concrete
Rises and falls as cars come and go
Their lights pulling across my ceiling
In an arc.

A siren pushes through
Sweeping up to the light
And then gone,
the echo left hanging
over the courthouse.

Somebody is walking a dog.
Somebody is pushing a stroller,
shushing a tired toddler.

And all I hear is the wind.

A Forest for the Trees

One of the things you take for granted when you ride a New York subway train is the clutter of cardboard advertising that rings the ceilings and surrounds the doors. On the one hand, it's great that advertising subsidizes commuting costs and helps to keep the cost of public transportation down, but on the other, sitting there or standing there, you can get the idea that you just aren't doing all that well because the vast majority of the signs promote betterment. You poor guy, get better by doing this thing I'm advertising up here.

This morning, I read ads for lawyers who want you to think they can net you multiple millions if you just call their (888) number. CUNY bragged about their award-winning students. Former Mayor Bloomberg's last ditch effort to gut the soda pop industry was in evidence in many ads warning of the dangers of swilling too many sugary drinks. And the ever-present, ever-glowing Dr. Zizmor promised – via handwritten testimonials – that he could give you clearer skin. Every ad wanted you to do something, get better, do better, be better.

And there, at the back of the car on the F train to Queens, was a single poster from Poetry in Motion with a few lines from a poem by Jim Moore from *Love in the Ruins*. This familiar series of poetry installations on the subway was reinstated in 2012 – because New Yorkers asked for it. It's sponsored by the MTA and a group called Arts for Transit that helps to bring music, art, sculpture, and poetry to New York City trains and stations.

But what a tremendous impact poetry has when you are surrounded by swirling ads for speedy food delivery and technical school programs. It was like seeing the forest for the trees. Peeping out over the head of a guy with headphones and a messenger bag was a single poster with just a few beautiful lines. I could swear there was a faint but distinct whiff of Lily of the Valley, a slowing of motion that was like someone placing a comma in the running noise and distraction of that train ride, speeding from stop to stop.

I was remembering my mother this week. She died two years ago Tuesday. There are days now when I don't think about her so much, but I still quote her all the time. She was beautiful, she was important, and my God, she was smart. And Jim Moore's words in the midst of all that advertising reminded me to refresh my thoughts and reboot my morning.

I saw a poster again today – but this time, someone had edited the poem. There was another handwritten line Sharpied on the sign after each printed line. New York subway riders are all editors at heart.

I'm sure there are lots of people who can exit the train without realizing what just happened. Maybe they jot down the number for Apex Tech and make that call to that 800 number that changes everything and makes them better. Still, even without that better job or clearer skin or an award for being something wonderful at CUNY, you could just be better for reading a poem.

Growing Pumpkins in the Bronx

It's funny the things you don't pay attention to when you are on your way to the bus. Most mornings, I'm on some kind of auto-pilot. If you asked me how I got to the bus stop, I would probably stammer something about crossing the street, or stopping at the corner and looking both ways. The details would typically escape me. I keep my head down and just get there somehow.

A couple of weeks ago, I noticed something. In an empty tree well on one of the side streets in the neighborhood, I noticed weeds. Weeds grow everywhere so noticing weeds is like noticing stop lights. They're there, so what, move along. But these weeds were big and big weeds are not common, at least not around here. Somebody usually comes along and cleans them out.

These big weeds became how I started my day. I'd walk out the back door, swing by the weeds, see how they were doing, and move on down the street to catch my bus. In just a short while, they were eye-high and I found myself looking forward to seeing them, to catching up with them.

"How're you doing, weeds?"

"I'm eye-high, how're you?"

I checked in with the porter who was taking out the trash bags the other day. I asked her if there was something special about these particularly large weeds, if someone was going to clean the little plot they were growing in, if she knew what kind of weeds they were, and if those really were squash blossoms. I fully expected to find out they were about to be mown, if that's the word for taking out the weeds and leaving the little square empty again.

"Those are Joe's pumpkins."

Well, of course, that's what they are! And that would explain the squash blossoms.

"Oh. Have a nice day."

"You, too."

The next morning, I ran into him. Joe is the superintendent in this building. Had he really planted pumpkins in a three by four foot empty tree well in this street in the Bronx?

"These your pumpkins?"

In fact they were. He planted them.

He told me the tall red weeds in the middle were something the "Indian People" liked for lunch. Apparently, Indian people had been harvesting the stalky things and leaving his pumpkin plants alone. It didn't look like rhubarb so I was at a loss in my attempt to identify it. He was fascinated that anyone would want them. Keep in mind, they were growing in the street.

But alas, there weren't any pumpkins for all those huge blossoms. Joe explained that the pumpkins usually grow right behind the blossoms but this year, nothing. Strong, beautiful blooms, but not one pumpkin. He was clearly disappointed.

The next day, the tiny plot was empty. The stalks, the blossoms, the weeds were all gone. There were the usual bits and pieces of flotsam and jetsam, the stuff you see on the street. In the place of squash blossoms and stalky things, there was a simple, plain rectangle of dirt and debris. You'd never know that his garden had been there.

This is just a footnote, a subset of what happens every day in a big city. He had planted pumpkin seeds, he had looked after this tiny garden, some random stalks had appeared that became lunch for the Indian people, and in the end, there were no pumpkins and the whole exercise was cleared away.

What makes this extraordinary is that while everyone knows a tree grows in Brooklyn, not too many people know that pumpkins could be growing in the Bronx.

Planting Allegheny Serviceberries in NYC

I guess you could say that it all started in the Bronx. I had heard about the Million Tree initiative that was started under Mayor Bloomberg but I had no personal experience with it. Until last week, when I spotted this new tree.

I had noticed this very tree well last fall, when my super planted pumpkin seeds there in the hopes of growing and harvesting his crop. The spot lay fallow for a scant few months and then, this hearty little tree appeared smack dab where the pumpkin plants were but the actual pumpkins were not.

It's got a tag that says, "I am one in a million." And it refers to the program to plant one million – seriously, million – trees in New York City. Being the skeptic that I am, I fully expected the trees to line the already tree-full streets of the Upper East and Upper West Sides of Manhattan where the more politically inclined citizens live. I figured this tree thing was only a way to pay back even further the political clubs in town that had supported Michael Bloomberg's many, many, many campaigns for mayor.

I could not have been more wrong, and those of you who know me know I do not admit that lightly. This little tree in the Bronx is only the tip of a rather ambitious iceberg going on now the weather has let up just enough to plant something.

On Monday this week, I was walking through Long Island City – a sad little part of the borough of Queens – and I saw the street was blocked by a flatbed truck that had about a dozen, maybe 14 trees lying on their side, their roots wrapped in burlap. I asked the guy standing next to the truck what was up with the trees and he said, "These are the city trees that are part of the million tree program."

These trees are such a godsend to Long Island City and to the Bronx. If there ever was something I would want my tax dollars to buy, it has to be trees.

They've all still got their training wheels on – you know, those stakes they plant on either side of the trunk so the new little tree doesn't fall right over. And they get cute little paper name tags that remind you where they came from – The City. These are Allegheny Serviceberry trees. They even have red or green silicon wristbands on lower branches that number them in the series so you can establish birth order.   The tags also tell you how to care for this lovely foundling. It's like finding a kitten in a basket on your doorstep: "Where'd you come from, cutie? Oh, mom, can we keep her? Please, please?"

In so many ways, there is no more forlorn section of the city than this part of Long Island City in Queens. It has warehouses, garages, vacant lots, and lots of traffic. But now, it's also got trees. Lots of new, little trees. Earnest, healthy, free trees. And the best part is this: next spring, these babies will be wearing flowers in their hair, so songbirds will love them too.

I hope The City keeps that tree truck guy busy for a very long time.

The Bench

I stopped in front of our bench today,
Remembering you sitting there.

I would sit next to you,
Watching the dogs pull on a leash
The skaters
The children
The couples holding hands.
You would lean in
And I would smile
Feeling calm.

Then we'd talk,
Clever with the double-entendres
Provocative,
Speaking a language only we knew.

But the bench is empty now
And I miss the banter.

Even now, after all that, you are still
My physics,
My reflex,
My answers.

I'll sit here a while.

How is she?

The Life of a Squirrel

I was on the bus this morning, on the way to my second bus to work, when I saw something move across the tree on the corner. Typically nothing out the window catches my eye because it's so much the same every day, but this time I watched as two crazy in love squirrels chased each other around the thick branches, ducking in and out of sight as if they were playing hide and seek. That's what squirrels do in mating season.

Squirrels are everywhere in New York. Most people call them rats with bushy tails. But suddenly, I needed to know more about squirrels so I did about two minutes' worth of research on them and found out a couple of interesting squirrel facts. One is that late winter is indeed their mating season, but most adult squirrels live alone. Their life expectancy is on average around six years and more city squirrels die dodging cars than by reaching the ripe old age of six. Country squirrels are more likely to die when they can't find enough food. They live on nuts and berries, which I knew, and their name is derived from Greek, meaning "one who lives in the shadow of their tail."

So I wondered this morning what it's like to be a squirrel. There I was on my way to my office with the same emails and reports and phone calls and irritations I had yesterday or the day before, and here were these two amorous squirrels just chasing each other around the tree. I knew pretty much everything that would happen in my own next hour, but these little critters were completely free to script theirs. They could chase, or make love, or hunt for nuts together and then do it all over again or just curl up inside that tree and nap, tails entwined together.

What they do not know is that their life expectancy is only six years, assuming they are successful crossing the street later today. That is such a different way to go about business, not knowing your life expectancy. Maybe they think they are immortal or that it's only cars that stand in the way of their living forever. Maybe they know that they need to make the most of the day, or maybe they just take the next hour at face value. I can't be certain, but I think taking an hour on squirrel terms might be preferable sometimes to my knowing everything about the next hour.

They say that listening to familiar music is calming because you can predict the outcome. If you hear the opening few bars of Beethoven's *Fifth Symphony* or *God Bless America*, you relax because you know where it's going. For the next few minutes, you won't be caught off guard or surprised. That's why the musical comedian Peter Schickele was such a hit with classical music lovers in the 1970s. We all thought we knew where the music was going, so when Schickele, AKA PDQ Bach, took us in with the familiar and then led us down another musical path, it was hilarious because it did catch us off guard. He would start a familiar classical tune and end up somewhere in *Yankee Doodle* or *Happy Birthday*. In some small way, he taught us not to relax, not to predict, not to rely on experience or habit. Stay in the moment and see where it leads you.

But today, the Ash Wednesday admonition is running in the back of this observation – the blessing about being dust and returning to dust. It's one of the reasons I don't like any part of that ash process. I prefer not to be reminded of my mortality today. I want to be like those two squirrels. They don't know what the day has to offer other than they have blue skies, their own tree, and each other for comfort and warmth. Today is a day for squirrels. They don't know cars will kill them if they aren't fast enough and they don't know they will likely not see their seventh year. They just know what's in front of them today and that they need nuts to survive. No bills, no mortgage, no complicated family obligations, few worries other than their nut supply, and nobody expects them to do much.

In many ways, I live in the shadow of my tail too, and today, for just the duration of a bus ride from the Bronx to Manhattan, I wanted to live the life of a squirrel.

Up All Night

Burst into bloom,
Didn't see it.
Explode into color,
No, missed it.
Flowering, blooming, blossoming.
Sorry. I just wasn't there.

When I walked past yesterday
There was green
All green, just leaves, nothing to see
Until now and you stop me cold.

Blood red blooms, hiding just behind
All green, just leaves,
nothing to see
Just didn't notice before.

I watched you die last summer,
Brittle petals falling away.

But now
Blood red blooms
leaning off the slender stalk.

Are you going to last?
No.

Did anyone see you?
No.

Was anyone witness?
Hear the explosion?
Catch the dust?
See the first bloom of this thing?!

A Marshmallow on the Bus

No.
Not unless you were
    up all night.

Is It Time for a Bucket List?

Is it time for a bucket list?

I always associate bucket lists with people dying. It's from that Jack Nicholson movie. You wander around checking things off a list, getting things done, getting happy, and then you die.

So, what makes me think today is the day to put my own list together? I'm not sure the reasons are all that compelling to read, so I'm just going to set down my list. Maybe if I do this, I'll be forced to take a better look at all the stuff I should be doing instead of making lists.

In no particular order, much as I am a neat and organized person by nature, this is what I want to do:

- To learn how to sail a boat. I love pirate stories and my dad won trophies for sailing.
- To take a selfie on the Great Wall of China. I saw a Turkish Airlines ad where Leonel Messi and Kobe Bryant did that and I think that's pretty neat.
- To photograph Stonehenge on a solstice, any solstice. I bet you can feel the cosmic energy.
- To walk the Camino de Santiago from Paris. I have only walked from Sarria and León.
- To see a play I have written performed in a theater that sells tickets and souvenirs.
- To meet the Pope.
- To find the graves of my ancestors in Canada, Ireland, England, France, and Germany.
- To walk on the upper gallery of Notre Dame Cathedral in Paris. Did you know they used to say Mass up there?
- To achieve lifetime membership at Weight Watchers. Lifetime members are my heroes.

- To attend a bullfight. My daughters are huge fans, but I am never in Spain in bullfighting season.
- To attend the men's finals at the Paris Tennis Open.
- To see the final match of the soccer World Cup – not necessarily in Brazil. I can wait.

That's about it. By my count, I just delayed getting to this list by about 12 minutes.

Ciao!

Worrying the Rubik's Cube

I changed buses this morning in front of the Twin Donut Shop, same as always, hopping off the first bus just in time to make the second for my ride to work. I paid the fare, took a seat on the right, not too far from the driver, and found myself looking into the face of a man who looked like he had just won the lottery. He was holding a Rubik's cube; the hottest toy of the 1980s.

So I was intrigued. I had planned to read my book for the next 20 minutes but I couldn't take my eyes off him. He was mid to late 40s, dressed for the weather, carrying a public television canvas bag, like the ones you get in the mail after you've made a donation. And he had this intense, full-face smile. Typically, on a New York City bus, that means only one of two things: you are on drugs, or you are certifiably insane, but nothing else about him supported either of these conclusions. So I thought, maybe he was using the cube the way some people carry worry beads. I thought maybe he was finding his early morning bliss in turning it around and around, over and over again.

The bus moved along, stopping every few blocks to drop off and pick up commuters, and he kept worrying the cube. I could see that the colored paper stickers that cover each of the small flat plastic pieces were frayed at the edges, like he had used this particular cube many times. He looked at it and turned it and looked at it again and the pattern of looking and turning started to look familiar to me. My daughters solve the cube, one even competing in timed solving events. This is how you do it. You establish which color sits in the middle, the only one that does not turn, and you marry up the rest of the same color to match it. It's not simple, but there is a set pattern of turns that will net you a solved cube every time.

By the next stop, he'd solved it. With one short toss in the air, he caught the cube and slipped it into his pocket. A second later, he was reading a book from the public television bag and nobody getting on the bus at the next stop would have known he was a cuber. And a particularly happy one at that.

We got off the bus together and got our coffee from the same cart on the corner. I wanted to let him know I'd watched him solve it, but I kept thinking of the stickers and how worn they were. Solving the cube this morning would have been a big deal for me, but for this man, it was just something to occupy his thoughts on a bus ride to work. And it made him so very happy.

Just Chatting

A tall, slim brunette waits for the M4 bus at 157th Street and Broadway. She's on the phone.

"Oh, look, there's the limited – shoot, I really wanted to get a donut. Oh well. Give me a second."

"Excuse me, I'm sorry. Pardon me."

"OK, where was I? How *are* you? I know, it was raining when I left my house, too. You know, I never think to bring my umbrella until after the stupid rain stops. Right, me too. I got a new rain hat, by the way, it's kind of new, I guess. It was on sale at Marshall's. Yeah, I don't get down there as often as I would like either. I get to Old Navy, you know, the one on Sixth Avenue? I love that Old Navy. You do? You know, I never fell in love with the layout of that 34th Street store. My daughter knows a girl from high school who works there. She *does* get a discount, but it's not so much, I don't think."

"You know, I was in a store over the weekend trying on bags. They had the most wonderful shoulder bags so I asked the guy behind the counter if he got a discount, you know, just joking with him. He said he did, but he had to wait a year to get it. Imagine that. No, I didn't buy the bag. It was really nice, but I decided it was just too expensive. No, these bags *never* go on sale."

"I liked your bag, that dark purple one you had yesterday, is it new? I do that, too! Whenever I switch over from one bag to the next, I always forget something. Your MetroCard? That's a bummer. Can I float you some quarters when I get into the office? Wow, you *are* prepared. I never have quarters when I need them. I used to collect them when the laundry room in my building had those old machines, the ones that took quarters? But now, they use the little plastic cards so I never have quarters anymore. No, you're right. I'm still dropping off my clothes at that little place, the one by the new gym. No, I haven't been in there yet, but my friend joined and she goes. It's only $15 a month if you take the plan without the trainer. I know, *I'd* need a trainer. Maybe that's what stops me from going. Well, that and the fact I don't want strangers watching me on a treadmill. That's a little weird. Oh. I never thought of that! Of course, they'll be watching the TV. OK, so I don't have an excuse now, do I?"

VOICE: *Next stop, 145th Street. Please exit using the rear doorway.*

"Did you see they closed the little dress shop place by the donut place, the one next to that fish place, you know the one. I never went in there. You don't think that's why they closed, do you? Right, right. Anyway, I was just telling Betty the other day, you just never see little dress shops anymore."

"I have so much respect for people who open shops. I wouldn't know the first thing. How to order supplies, manage bank deposits, staff the place, day in, day out? And pretty much none of these folks are native New Yorkers either. I think they probably come from other places where their families had stores. Maybe that's it."

VOICE: *Next stop, 137th Street. Please exit using the rear doorway.*

"Oh, say, they reopened that old theater across the street on Broadway. Yeah, that one. I can't believe it went from being a theater to a discount place, to that furniture place, do you remember that one? To a doctor's office? That's remarkable. And wow, they have a cool second floor to it, too. Oh shoot, I just dropped my sunglasses case. Well, they said the rain was going to stop by lunch time. Give me a second. How's your book coming? That's great. I can loan you another one from my book club, if you want something. I never know what to do with them when I'm done with them. You just run out of space. I forgot you have that Kindle. I'm just not ready for it. I know I could carry my whole library with me. I don't know."

VOICE: *Next stop, 125th Street. Please exit using the rear doorway.*

"Did you see? That restaurant, the old Cuban place, reopened a couple of weeks ago. It's right over there under the thing, next to the barbecue place? Yeah. I haven't been there yet. It's not as convenient as their old location, but to be honest, I didn't go there that often either. I did like the food."

"Yeah, we can get lunch. What's your schedule like, I don't know, Thursday? Thursday's good? OK, cool. I'll send you an email when I get into my office. They make great pork sandwiches. I do remember that. Oh, gotta hang up now, I'm here. I'll see you in five. OK, Bye!"

VOICE: *Next stop, 116th Street. Please exit using the rear doorway.*

"Thank you, driver, have a great day!"

"Thanks. Have a nice weekend, Cathy!"

The River

I am the pioneer,
not you.

When you came, I had already seen
the vast stretches of tall cool grass and trees shading,
standing,
watching.

When you came,
I had already known
the warmth of late summer twilight
and the chill of an early fall sunrise.

I am the pioneer,
not you.

I washed over your tired feet and soothed your limbs
and your pain
I was there to refresh you and I watched you smile at
the taste of my
clear water.

Do you remember the quiet winter when you skated
across my frozen surface,
shouting and laughing with your friends?

And then the spring,
when you built little boats
and I tossed you in them?

I am the pioneer,
not you.

I washed over my banks over and over again and you
said I didn't know where to stop.

A Marshmallow on the Bus

I flooded the hills and the paths
over and over again
and you thought I was wrong,
that you could fix me.

I came up to your silly bridges
and lapped against the fragile wood structures
you buried in my riverbed.
I'll win you know.

I carried away your simple tents and your plantings
and playthings
And you.

I carried you all on my back down stream
until nobody remembered
you,

But you will remember me.

You will say,
      "The spring of aught-six was
      a bad one, the river was a terrible thing,"
and you will fear me now,
      you will run from me
and you will move your tents away
and you will have to bring my water
up hills to your homes.

And I will miss the time
when I washed over your feet
and you sat along my banks,
sipping my clear water.

It's different now.
It's my nature that you should
fear me.

A Marshmallow on the Bus

I am the pioneer.
Not you.

Subway History in the Subway Stairs

Most subway stations in New York have a similar palette. White tiles, grey cement floors, the yellow edge of the platform, and all those shiny silver trains. Many stations have mosaics dating from the first few years of the 20th century and some have nice new ones – dating from the 1990s; like the 81st Street Station on the B and C lines or the 66th Street Lincoln Center station on the 1 line. But this station, the Rockefeller Center station where the B, D, F, and M lines stop, has something wonderful that not only adds to the color palette but also gives a glimpse of the station's past where you might least expect it.

The staircase hand railings at the far end of the platform, unlike so many staircases in the New York subway system, are made of wood. It has been painted over and over again in what I think is about four different colors, the last of which is a high gloss black. But underneath, as the paint wears away, there is a rust color, a vibrant yellow, and a flat utilitarian tan. And each color is visible as the color on top of it wears off.

A metal stair rail runs alongside the wooden one and this time of year, it will chill you to use it. I'd like to say the wood one warms to the touch, but it doesn't and in both cases, you will find your hands colder at the bottom of the stairs here than they were at the top, assuming you use the stair rails like I do.

Someone took the time to carve a few letters here, a name there, and at the bottom of this staircase, where the paint is completely gone and only the varnished wood remains, you'll see the name "Ken."

But I love the palette; that multicolored, Jackson Pollock, paint splash of colors from what is probably 80 years' worth of paint. It covers the wear inflicted on that railing every day by tens of thousands of cold hands in the winter, sweaty hands in the summer. We have worn our way down to the rust-colored paint here, down to the yellow paint there, to the tan over there, and finally, to the original varnish. The last person who varnished that stair rail could have been the artist who installed it when the station opened, coinciding with the construction of Rockefeller Center in 1930.

The metal railing that runs next to it was probably installed just to meet some city code. It would surprise me if this wooden stair rail were removed any time soon though, because it is just as solid as the newer metal railing. It could use a fresh coat of paint – which normally I would applaud. But not here. When the painters come in to cover this railing again, probably with a fresh coat of that high gloss black, I will miss the colors and the small view into Rockefeller Center's past.

Bus Surfing in Manhattan

You should notice her right away.

It's 80 degrees, it's humid for this time of year, everyone is shifting their weight, looking for a bit of shade, a little breeze, and it's early, so the day will be warmer in no time.

But she's wearing a quilted winter coat. It's got long sleeves with close knitted cuffs, buttoned to her chin, the hood lying limp and flat against her back. Most of these people just aren't paying any attention to her. They are waiting for a bus that should have come long ago and nobody's interested in this woman.

And a hat.

She's wearing a hat and it's dark, knitted with some kind of fuzzy yarn like mohair or angora, and it covers her hair like a snood. The hat is a heavy, out of season signal that there is something wrong, something not right. How could she have thought today was the day for this quilted coat, this suffocating hat?

She's at the bus stop and she smiles at the man standing next to her, the one with the pork pie hat. She's trying to get his attention. That's how she does it. A deliberate smile goes out, a reflex kind of smile or a nod goes back, and she's hooked you. She reels you in, making you think it's all about the small talk of waiting for the bus here on this corner.

"Looks like rain." She starts. "Should have brought my umbrella."

"I always forget mine." He smiles. "Should just leave it in my bag, right?"

Smiling, congenial. Now they're acquaintances, closest friends. They share something, have something in common, have a conversation going. She can keep talking long enough to look like she belongs. But she doesn't belong. These people are going places, but she's not going anywhere really.

She's a rider. She'll get on and stay on, hoping nobody notices she just never gets off.

He steps aside as the bus pulls up to the stop, gesturing to let her on the bus just ahead of him.

"Ladies first," he tells her, as she climbs in. She stops, standing just next to the fare box. He notices the fuzzy hat, pays his fare and walks into the center of the bus.

"Driver?" she asks. "Does this bus stop at Penn Station?"

"Yes, ma'am, it does."

"Can you give me an idea of how long it will take to get there?" she asks.

"Probably close to 45 minutes," he responds, not looking at her now, but watching the steady stream of passengers board and pay their fares. She steps to the side.

There are mothers taking children to school, or daycare, then they will go on to work. Some high school girls are next, comparing photos on their phones, whispering about the boys, making plans. Everyone is clearly grateful for the air conditioning on the bus and the quick flush of cold air on their faces and the back of their necks.

"Looks like rain, right, driver?"

She has slowly, imperceptibly, edged around to the opposite side of the fare box, her body now closer to the empty front seats just behind him.

"Yes, ma'am, I guess it does."

Then she slips right by him. Does he notice she never paid her fare? She has just dissolved into the chill, disappeared. She looks right at the man from the street corner, but he has already buried his face in his book, not to speak with her again. The jig is up. He's on to her. He knows her game and she can't use him anymore.

The bus pulls away from the curb and she makes her way to the very last seat in the back, smiling slowly and deliberately at every rider in turn. There's just one man sitting there, nearest the window, holding a neatly folded free newspaper. He looks relieved to be in the cool air of this bus. To her, he's fresh meat.

She takes the seat directly opposite him.

"Looks like rain, right?"

Days, Dates, and Places

I remember why I left you,
you thief.

You were everything and nothing I ever wanted,
but I needed you so.

And now, I remember the days, dates,
and places of us,
        and not the sense.

"Little, by little," Kate told me, "You'll forget him."
And I did, mostly.

I remember the bridge we looked for all night,
but not the full view of it.
I remember the plaid shirt you left on the bed,
but not the sweet scent of it.
I remember the laughing, the playing, the shouts,
but not the high sound of it.
I remember the sand and the water and the fish,
but not the salt touch of it.
I remember you feeding me, offering me Scotch,
but not the tart taste of it.

How is it the calculated traces of you
are so clear to me now, but not the sense?

At first, I wanted to remember it all,
but little by little, she was right, I forgot.

        I forgot why I fell for you,
        but I remember why I left you, you thief.

Stupid Rain: A Sad Little Poem

Stupid rain.
Don't wake me up with your stupid
crashing splashing.
Stay off my sidewalk, stay off my windows,

And if you must make a soggy visit,
For God's sake, do it quiet like.

Those folks you hear touting long,
romantic walks in the rain?
Ignore them.
They are fools.

Smart people know to come in out of the rain.
Smart people shut the windows
and ignore the rain.

Why, I remember the summer I was in France
And there was this town
And they never got rain in the summer
And I thought they were blest.
I wanted to stay.

Rain drives me indoors.
I read, I nap, I snack,
I hibernate,
And not once do I wish
I could take a long walk in the rain.

I did that once.
Six hours, pouring rain,
And me walking in it.
Nevermore.

The Tin Can Emporium

Sadly, I'm not taking as many buses these days as I used to. I've gone from a four bus a day commute to a six train and, all of a sudden, it's like I'm a tourist in my own town. It is not a difficult route, and if I time it just right, I walk off one train onto another and keep moving. It's about 40 minutes each way.

What I am noticing now are all the little markets that open just for an instant in well-timed, brilliantly choreographed commerce on the train. This is just a random sample of the vendors I've seen on trains:

1) Mariachi band. These guys are pretty wonderful. I have seen probably a half dozen different Mariachi bands in the past, say, five years of so. Typically it's a guy with a guitar, maybe a guy with an accordion, or two guys with guitars. They sing in harmony and their song lasts the length of one stop so they can collect some money and scoot out to the next car before the train leaves the station again.

2) DVD seller. There are two guys and one woman – I think they're a team – who sell DVDs by walking with some haste from one end of the car to the other, displaying their plastic cases with copies of movies that either just opened in theaters or are about to open. I think I read once that selling them is the crime, not buying them. But they remind me of the time I bought one of *The Lion King* years ago to satisfy my kids who were not happy waiting for the official Disney copy to come out. In the middle of the first scene with Scar, you could watch as somebody crossed in front of the copy guy's handheld camera to go get popcorn. Modern DVD copy guys are much more sophisticated.

3) Famous Amos' Chocolate Chip Cookies Guy. This is really a good market, all in all. These guys buy huge boxes of snacks and cookies at discount stores like BJ's or Costco and then sell the packages individually for a dollar. Given they probably only pay around 25 cents apiece for what they sell, the markup is pretty good. This week, I watched a guy

who started his spiel with "I'm not stealing, I'm just dealing a little candy here on the train and if you ain't smiling I can get you some snacks." Or something like that.

He had, in two cardboard boxes that were lashed together with plastic tape, Welch's fruit snacks, Snickers bars, Famous Amos cookies, and Pringles chips. I watched him kneel down in front of the woman seated next to me as she asked for Welch's Berries and Cherries and a pack of Famous Amos. He looked at her in judgment, remarkably, and asked her, "You want both?" It wasn't confirmation. It was judgment, as if he were telling her, "One snack per person this close to dinnertime is plenty, miss."

4) Break dancers. There are a couple of groups of break dancers that I see regularly; one group in particular that really irritates me. They set their boombox in the middle of the aisle and start clapping really loud. They dance – which most folks can't see, given the way seats are configured on a train – and then one of them swings up, holding the pole, and slams his open hand with a sharp smack against the ceiling of the train. After that, they pass the hat and get out so they can repeat the performance in the next car.

5) The box lady. There is a woman I have seen a couple of times who kneels down with a cardboard box and sings. She has a personal tale of woe and it always rhymes with the word "box" in some fashion. She bangs on the box and then asks for money.

6) The comedian. On the #1 train, there used to be a guy who did stand-up on the train. He had a routine about his fat wife and he always ended the bit with something like, "Pick up after yourselves as you exit the train. I've got company coming over later." I haven't seen him in a while – I hope he's OK.

7) Evangelists. These people tend to offend rather than persuade. The last one I saw spent his moment in the spotlight trying to convince everyone that gays go to hell. As you can imagine, everyone on the train piped up to shout him

down. It was one of the more interactive moments in all this commerce.

What fascinates me is both the speed with which business is conducted on a moving subway train and the careful timing that has to take place to make sure you, as the seller, don't get caught in the same train car for two stops. That is particularly awkward – you've exhausted your repertoire and your audience at the same time, yet there you stand, waiting for the door to open at the next stop so you can get back to business by hopping off one car and scuttling across the platform to jump into the next train car before the doors close. That happens rarely, but it is interesting to watch how terribly uncomfortable they look.

About a year ago, there was a group of women and a little boy sitting just across from me when one of the regular sellers came over to them selling small plastic toys. The boy saw the man but before he could go into his act, the boy started shouting at him.

"One dollah, one dollah, one dollah!"

And the whole car started to laugh. The boy sounded just like the toy guy.

All on the Way to Work

Foggy today. The temperature is higher now than whatever normal is these days and the air was thick with the anticipation of rain or a cold front or something that was still taking form this morning as I walked out to catch my bus.

Coats are darker now, too. There was one woman walking toward me with a crayon red shopping bag swinging alongside her, but other than that, it was just so many shades of black.

Coffee drinkers were everywhere and, out in the street, pulling slowly up to the corner, a short-ish woman tugged on a shopping cart that trailed behind her. It was full, no, wait, it was overflowing with empty bottles and cans. Piled high over her head, to twice her height, she had collected what looked like a half dozen body bag-sized clear plastic bags' worth of empties.

At this hour, she was either out all night, collecting and sifting through trash cans and street bags or she had this massive *objets trouvés* in her apartment overnight. I wondered how you would go about protecting a stash like this if you ever let it out of your sight. If I calculate correctly, I would imagine you could feed your family for a week on the returns from this many bottles and cans.

My bus left her trudging toward the big supermarket down the street.

At the bus stop on Broadway, I decided to take the train downtown. There's construction on the corner near my office now and the bus doesn't let out anywhere near me so the train is just as good. I figure, if I have to walk anyway, I might as well get there quicker, right?

Train etiquette in the morning rush is an unwritten code. Step over the feet lollygagging in the aisles, ignore the guy taking two seats, don't bump into the short people holding the poles near the door, and if somebody gets on with a cane or a pair of crutches, stand up and make a big grand deal of relinquishing your seat. I took it all in and kept to myself.

Ten minutes later, I stepped out into the fog again.

It is still so thick I can barely see Grant's Tomb. The Memorial is wrapped in this silky fog and the memory of the man they say saved the Union. There's a jogger, running up the block, cutting through the haze. She's got a pink Day-Glo headband.

An Unremarkable Day

Some days, it doesn't pay to get out of bed. I used to hear that a lot and I always wondered if it were true. It might be age, it might be the season, being pre-spring and all, and it just might be my irritating sunny disposition, but I think life pays to get out of bed even if you only have an unremarkable day to show for yourself at the end of the day.

Today was an unremarkable day. I tapped the snooze button on my phone alarm and had every intention of going back to sleep for 10 minutes but ended up checking my mail, my Facebook account, my Twitter feed, the *New York Times* app, the weather, and LinkedIn just to see what was waiting for me. No extra sleep, but I felt that I had actually multi-tasked enough to be ahead of the game.

I found my girls had made coffee but it smelled like hazelnut so I made a Nespresso and toasted an unfrosted strawberry Pop Tart and sat down to watch *The Today Show*. *The Today Show* gang has not been the same since they relieved Ann Curry of her NBC contract, so I swap back and forth to MSNBC and CNN to compare newsy bits and then take a shower. I am out the door a few minutes later to catch my buses to my office.

Everyone was predicting snow today, but I grew up in Michigan so I didn't pay any attention. I spent the morning in my office working on a spreadsheet that's due the end of next week and when folks got chatty outside my door, I cranked up my favorite banjo music and smiled. I cannot complain if it's going to snow and I have banjo music. Things went well with the spread so I met a good friend at lunch time and we talked for the longest time about some office things before I stopped into a local Chinese place for takeout fried rice.

This afternoon, I was able to finish the spreadsheet to the point where I could move into the next phase of the project, confirming that all the data is correct, so I turned back on the banjo radio station and kept at it until a very friendly tech guy came in to help me restore all my recently lost email archives. For some reason, last Thursday, all my saved messages went down the proverbial E-drain. I got them back this afternoon and now I have no excuse for not answering lots of questions, like "what did he say he wanted to teach?" Or, "when did she say she wanted to take that course off?" Piecing together next year's curriculum at an Ivy League university is a pretty complicated exercise and I will still be finalizing the data next week.

But looking back now at all of these small accomplishments, I have to recognize that even though this was a truly unremarkable day, I did quite a bit and I should acknowledge that. I got up on time, I was able to make my own breakfast, I had hot water for my shower, and I caught my two buses – both right on time. That's not bad. Then, I worked in a heated office with my friends and colleagues only a phone call away, I was able to listen to my banjo music and I didn't spill anything into my keyboard. That's not bad either. And wonder of wonders, it turned out I had backed up the emails to my external hard drive correctly and there they were, hiding, just waiting to go back home to my email account.

I am not sure if I need to make a real point here, but it would probably look something like this: if you can sleep in a clean place, have enough to eat, work in a safe place, and have friends who will listen to you, it probably wasn't an unremarkable day, all in all. I came home and my son made me dinner. That was enough to move this unremarkable day into the misty realm of a great day.

Gloves Gloves Gloves!

This morning, I had errands to run. Not my typical commute to Manhattan at all. I dropped off my dry cleaning at the place where they read the Bible all day in Korean and my laundry at the little place out the back door that's painted orange. Then I caught my regular bus number one near the train station in the Bronx.

Since I needed to go farther downtown than usual today, I changed at Broadway to the train. Nothing out of the ordinary here at all, but when you are riding any form of New York City transit, in some way, everything is out of the ordinary. What I love is how small incidents can appear and then disappear with the most alarming speed.

I board the train and stand in the center, but only about three feet from the doors. The train pulls into the stop at 103rd Street and the woman whose seat I have been eyeing stands, steps past me, and walks out the doors as I pivot gracefully into her seat.

Then, I see two black stretchy gloves at my feet on the floor. Realizing they must have been hers and knowing I only had a few seconds to get them to her, I grab them up and start shouting "Gloves gloves gloves!" as I hear the fateful words on the intercom, "Stand clear of the closing doors, please."

She's not turning around, I'm still shouting, "Gloves gloves gloves" and the doors are about to close, so I did what any quick-thinking New Yorker would do, I tossed the gloves through the "closing doors," thinking someone either on or near the train will alert her that her gloves have arrived on the platform and that her cold hands are saved – along with her wallet, at not having to buy new gloves.

But, in an only-in-New-York flash, she turns, leans over to collect the gloves off the platform, and speaks: "So, you think it's alright to throw my gloves on the floor, do you?"

Then, I distinctly heard a grunt.

A Marshmallow on the Bus

Everyone near the door of the train starts to laugh and the doors close. The woman next to me leans over and says the immortal words, "No good deed, right?" To which I respond, "She was probably just upset she didn't catch them."

I am no expert on how long trains typically stay in any given station during rush hour, but my guess is, on the local, not more than 10 to 15 seconds, give or take. That was all it took for her to stand, me to sit, me to see the gloves, me to grab the gloves and toss them out of the doors of the train, and her to grouse at me for doing it.

But everyone got a laugh. And the benefit from a laugh lasts much longer than 10 to 15 seconds.

Anger and the Standard of Contrition

There was a fight on my bus a few days ago. A woman in her late teens was standing in the front with a boy sitting in front of her who was two years old at the most. He was crying when I got on and she looked distracted, the way you look when you are watching for your stop. She leaned over him, grabbed the front of his jacket, picked him up about a foot off the seat, and dropped him back onto the seat, shouting, "Shut up!" A woman I couldn't see through the crowd, closer to the middle of the bus on the other side, shouted at her, "You can't treat a baby like that! You'll hurt him!" The mother shrieked back, "You can't tell me what to do with my baby!" The woman leaped out of her seat and attacked the mother, pulling her hair and punching her face, and the mother, ignoring the still crying baby, started beating the woman.

Then, the currently predictable things happened. Someone pulled out their phone to get it all on video, people moved away or closer to get a better view, until finally, a tall man in a parka separated the two by standing between them until the bus came to the next stop. Everyone emptied out of the bus in a hurry, expecting the driver to do something or call someone, but he didn't. He asked if everyone was alright and closed the doors to proceed to our next stop, as if nothing had happened.

I think a number of people on the bus did nothing to intervene because in their heart of hearts *they* wanted to punch that mother themselves for roughing up her child. The few moments we saw of her life with that child spoke volumes about them: if this was how she acted in public with him, who could guess what it was like without an audience?

I was disturbed by the level of rage that was present on a city bus filled with strangers. Here we all were on our way some place together but these women, the mother and the one who attacked her, were completely consumed by rage. This anger is something I see more often now and I'm

64

not sure why. It shows up when a cabbie cuts off a driver at an intersection or a delivery truck waits too long at a light to make a turn. And I see it on public transportation when one passenger or another sees something that does not meet their standard of courteous behavior, as in the case with the mother and her child on the bus. There is also the expectation that the offending party must be sufficiently contrite or suffer the consequences.

But this standard of contrition and courtesy, as false as it is, lays the foundation for anger that exceeds my standard of what is acceptable in any location. It's gotten to the point where I will avoid a particular bus route because the anger there is higher than other places. There are also times during the day when anger is highest and that, surprisingly to me, is during the morning commute. I'm more cautious and aware now in the morning.

Still, I worry about the future of that child, exposed not only to abuse by the mother, but also by adults everywhere in his daily life who exhibit what is fast becoming tolerable, acceptable rage. In this instance on my bus, the women involved were equally matched in terms of rage and aggression, but in many cases, these angry people are looking for the vulnerable, the innocent to attack in an effort to present themselves as the one in charge, the standard bearer for decent behavior. And in both cases, whether between the evenly matched or between an innocent and a bully, the rage that sparks the violent outcome is publicly tolerated. That's what you get, he had it coming. What did you expect me to do? Wait, let me get this on my phone.

Adrienne Rich said, in her poem *Peeling Onions*, "Only to have a grief equal to all these tears!" How is it that full-blown rage has come to be attached to these small exchanges on public transportation? It is wholly out of proportion to the offense. The mother was livid that someone would challenge her parenting skills. The woman was furious the mother didn't take her advice immediately. Both of them could have ignored the other and left the bus to go on with their day without incident.

Peace is an elusive thing. It is like a flag flapping high atop a pole, always out of reach. But anger and violence are never far from reach. Anger waits hidden from view, and in many ways, it is the most dangerous concealed weapon of all.

Adrienne Rich "Peeling Onions," Snapshots of a Daughter-in-Law (1963)

My Brave New Life

Everyone tries to be brave
To find courage or strength.
To go farther out, even out on a limb.
But for me, it's the sea.
I just need the sea.

How could I not have chosen this before?

To hear the songs of the sailors,
And let the salt in the air clear my head.
The shore birds shrieking out in the morning
Demanding more, more.
As they circle around me.

I am no longer a pilgrim at home.

My ship sits tall, brushing against the piers,
Barely stirring, softly moving
Creaking timbers, the ropes
Pulling against their moorings
Venus watching over the tall masts.

This port that greeted her
That steered her here
Lends me a gateway too.

I climb on board and lie flat out,
Dizzy from the swell and the clouds
Crossing overhead.
My fingers stretch to feel the broad deck.

Suddenly, she slips free, floating,
The sails filling, snapping,
Damp spray on my face,
My eyes close and I can feel the stars.

A Marshmallow on the Bus

And I am Mercury, facing the sun,
Leaving cold empty space behind me.

It's a gamble,
I'm out of time.
But it's no longer just a dream.
Standing now, I take my place with the crew,
And we scan the horizon together.

How could I not have chosen this before?

One Month on the Train: My MTA Journal

Since I think most people have never ridden a New York subway or walked to work in the city, I thought this might be a fun way for all you armchair travelers to see what my little commute looks like. This will be a random assortment of my observations – all on the way to work.

I started in the Bronx this morning, heading downtown on the D train to Rockefeller Center in midtown Manhattan. My doorman was cordial. You know, when we moved to the Bronx and my kids were faced with their first real doorman experience, it was a little challenging. They had been used to scooting out the front door, not a word to anyone, and now, they needed small talk.

"Good morning!"

"Good morning! Looks like it might snow again, right?"

"I don't know. Rafael Miranda – you know, that weather guy on Channel 4? – he didn't say anything about snow today, but maybe rain."

"Rain! Oh, OK, that's cool. Well, you have a good day."

"Thanks – you, too. See you later."

Still, I think we would all feel a little less connected without a doorman. He takes the place of neighbors in an urban apartment building. We don't talk to the neighbors. They bang on the ceiling when we are getting ready for bed and in the morning when I'm making coffee.

But the doorman? He just wishes us a nice day and opens the door.

A Marshmallow on the Bus

February 21 – I'm a Spy

Getting around during rush hour on the subway in New York City is all about knowing the rules. These are some of the more unwritten ones:

If you are standing near the door, you step out, still blocking the entrance, and you let new passengers push by you, all the while looking like a "guy" for stepping out.

If the free newspaper guys hand you a paper, you just take it.

If people are streaming up the stairs from a train that has just left, you wait to go down the stairs to the platform or you could get squished.

Those are the key elements I have learned in the month I have been on this new route in the morning.

But I hate routine. So, I have started hopping off my train at the station where I change from Train One to Train Two. I feel bold and liberated when I do it, like I am defying fate or throwing caution, as they say, to the winds. I scoot up the stairs, slide out through the turnstile and enter the concourse where there is an incredible maze of shops and donut places. I buy a French Vanilla Latte and feel like a spy collecting a briefcase full of documents from a designated drop.

The trick to the donut places however is that you have to know the rules there, too. You order in one line, pick up in another and God help you if you get that wrong. The folks waiting in line are on their routine and they just do not want any part of it interrupted by some girl who doesn't know the rules or worse, chooses to ignore them.

But some days, you just need that "I'm a spy" experience. And a French Vanilla Latte to go with it.

A Marshmallow on the Bus

February 24 – The Suits

This morning I watched as a thousand commuters got on the train – single, alone, selfishly listening to music, reading a book, or turning the pages of one of the free morning newspapers. It's a solitary business, going to work by train. Even if you see people you know, it's really difficult to coordinate your train with anyone else's train. If the train you agreed to ride together arrives a few minutes early, you will probably abandon your contact in favor of getting on the train. Conversely though, if it's late, I guess you would have someone to complain to, someone who would share your frustration.

It was really quiet this morning. I read my book – on my phone – and barely noticed that we had pulled into my switchover station as I now call it. I take one train and then switchover to another. It gives a chance to collect a fancy coffee sometimes and to suspend my route to Train Number Two for just a moment.

I did that today – I decided Monday was as good an excuse as you could get to buy a fancy coffee so I slid through the turnstile and out into the concourse where I stood and waited for that coffee. And I was suddenly surrounded by Suits – the men who dress alike in corporate America, who wear suits, and ties, and wing-tips. This is the first time, remarkably, that I have seen Suits in this spot. I overheard one of them as he threw his head back laughing – "Irish? Oh God, no, I grew up in an Italian neighborhood!" Hilarity all around.

What struck me immediately was not just the forced hilarity or them swapping stories about shoveling out their driveways, but how absent women were. This was a group of around a half dozen colleagues, all yucking it up about snow and their neighborhood, on their way to buy donuts, and for the life of me, I could not fathom how a woman would have fit into that picture this morning.

It's been a very long while since I was witness to such a 1950s, throwback view of the world of men and women. So, my Monday morning fancy coffee was soured because not only did I not find any way to see a woman fitting into this conversation, I realized that if I can't even imagine a way to buy donuts with these men, how do we ever find ourselves at that conference room table 10 minutes later, sharing donuts?

February 25 – What's For Breakfast?

This morning, lots of folks were eating breakfast on the train.

I got on and stood just behind a young man with the label still stuck to his baseball cap, announcing the size of the cap and the authenticity of the logo. He was holding a paper bag with a roll and an open bag of Doritos. In the time it took for us to get to the first express stop, he finished the Doritos, wiping orange dust off his wool scarf with his equally orange fingers. What a curious combination of foods – at any time, let alone for breakfast: a buttered toasted roll with Doritos.

On my second train, nearly everyone was involved with their headphones and the long white cables that tether them to their Smartphones, but one woman at the other end of the train was chasing down pills with water from a bottle that was so large it matched the length of her forearm.

Just across from me, an Asian woman carefully unwrapped a fluffy bun and pulled off pieces to eat while staring blankly at the windows of the train. She was carrying an orange Thermos – apparently, the color of the day. Watching this along with me was a younger woman who carried a coffee drink that was so large she nearly needed both hands. She dabbed a couple of times at her lips before blowing her nose into her napkin.

What an unsatisfying experience to eat your breakfast on the subway. All I could think of was my ideal, bucket list breakfast – a *café con leche* with an *ensaimada* at La Mallorquina on the Puerta del Sol in Madrid. Try it if you ever get there. It is my bliss.

February 26 – Parlez-vous enfer?

My children have the amazing ability to tell – at some distance – whether the train they hear as they enter the station is going uptown or downtown. This information is critical if you are either on a tight schedule or are worried the next arriving train won't come for 20 minutes. They know at a moment's listening whether they need to bolt through the turnstile and plummet down the stairs or take their time. As you might guess, I do not have this ability.

This morning, I entered the station and began the sloping walk to the entrance where you swipe in and just as I passed the door out to the street, I heard a train. I wished I had my kids with me so I could have known right there whether to run or just keep walking. It was only a moment later that I saw everyone streaking toward the platform and I decided that this morning, that dash was just not for me. I walked as everyone behind me sprinted.

But then, as I got to the turnstile everyone had sped through, I realized I could, in fact, make the train anyway and I took up the challenge and skittered down the stairs, just slipping through the "closing doors," as they are called.

I found myself standing next to a woman who had gotten on just ahead of me and we both heard the voice of the African-French preacher woman who frequents this train line in the morning. This morning she was speaking in French with only a few sentences in English and she kept repeating: "This is just for you, French speakers. Jesus loves you Jesus is the way the truth the life He died for you" – run-on, looping sentences with no discernible punctuation.

What was wrong with this? Other than the fact that most early morning train riders want silence accompanying them downtown, it's very likely only a half dozen or so of this train car's riders could understand a word she said – unless it was in English.

But I got the message. It was lovely, actually, that she would spend her commute waving the Bible at us, offering us the opportunity NOT to go to Hell today. But it was even more lovely when she got off at 125th Street in Harlem with her children and silence reigned.

February 27 – Homeless

This morning, there was what the voice on the loud speaker typically calls "an earlier incident" at a station uptown so the trains were running in funny ways to avoid the station with the incident. When I got off my Train One to switchover to Train Two, I was hit with the unmistakable fragrance of a vagrant. When I was a kid, the word was "bum." And when my mother was a kid, it was "hobo." Nobody uses the word vagrant much now, but that is the only word that sums up the wandering nature of a sleeping homeless man, wrapped in a worn comforter, sitting upright behind the stairs in a subway station during rush hour.

Seeing homeless people sleep in the subway is not remarkable – especially on a very cold and windy February morning. What caught my eye was his cart, or rather his system of carts that was parked up the platform from where he was sitting, just past my favorite staircase on the downtown D platform at the Rockefeller Center station.

This cart system of his was festooned with hearts. There were the typical plastic shopping bags filled with random debris, trash mostly, and a small plastic bucket at one end, but the face of it was hung or decorated with large red leftover Valentine's Day hearts. They did little to bring any sense of cohesion to the carts, which in total would have stretched about 8 to 10 feet out in front of him if he pushed it. Everyone walking by this morning gave it a look – few people saw him though because he was far enough away and tucked behind the stairs.

I think if I am ever so unfortunate as he, so desperately, terribly abandoned that I become homeless, I would hope I would have something this friendly on the front of my cart. But the one thing I think I can assure you is that my cart will be small with only a few paintings, musical scores, and photo albums.

Except for this one thing: nobody plans on becoming homeless. Of all of life's tragedies, it is the one that will haul off and smack you in the face, I think. I left hoping someone with more resources than I have will help him today be less homeless tomorrow.

February 28 – Hum with Me

It was quiet this morning on the trains. No giggly high school girls, no kids munching their breakfast, not a single loud-enough-to-bother headphone music spillover – nothing. I found myself in a car with roughly 80 other people and all I could hear was the metal against metal of the train as it moved down the track.

It's funny: you tend to notice the noise and not the quiet. The noise disturbs you, makes you look up, stops you in the middle of the page of your book. But the quiet is different. It seeps in and surrounds you and makes an artificial buffer around you that acts like a cocoon. You sit in your very own personal, self-constructed, enveloping cocoon, not touching anyone else's cocoon. And because there were so many of us on that one car, it was like pawns on a chessboard or chocolates in a box. Near, one to the other, but worlds away in silence. Like still life, what the French call "nature mort."

Then one rider interrupted the quiet. He got on at the express stop and apologized to me for stepping across my feet on his way to hold the center pole. He too was silent and I went back to my book. He was tall – tall enough to hold onto the top bar easily – and he carried a large navy blue duffel bag that he stowed between his feet.

And then he started humming. At first, I couldn't tell where the sound was coming from or who was making it, so I looked up. He wasn't wearing headphones like the kids who find themselves suddenly singing out loud to the music on their phones. But it was him. A sentence here, then silence again, as if he had forgotten the words. Then another sentence – humming too – and silence again.

When I got off, I missed hearing him sing. I never identified the song and I imagine he went on for several more stops, randomly singing a phrase here, humming a phrase there. It was as if one of the chocolates in this box, one of the pawns on this chessboard – one individual in a sea of sameness – he alone presented his individuality. We were all cocooned – he was the lone free agent.

And I was disappointed that the free agent this morning wasn't me. Not that I would sing on the train necessarily, but that I had stepped onstage into a scene in this morning's play that was already in progress and I did not want to create my own drama. When I used to take the bus, I would talk to other riders and the driver, making small talk about the weather or the traffic. I could challenge the environment. But now, on the train, I have become one of them. I'm a chocolate.

March 3 – Not in Service

By the time I got on the second platform to wait for my "switchover" train this morning, it was full. Passengers were streaming up from an earlier train, but the elusive F train was nowhere in sight. I heard the fateful 9 syllables over the loud speaker but recognized them not by sound but by cadence: "Because of an earlier incident, ..." What the incident was, where it had occurred, and how it would impact my life this morning remained a mystery.

But then, a train started to pull in and many of my fellow train customers this morning started moving toward the edge of the platform, getting ready to board. Instead of the regular F labeling on the face of the lead car though, the sign read "Not in Service." I can't remember the last time I saw that on a train because typically, when an entire train is out of service, it blares a horn on the way into the station and pulls though it slowly, not collecting any new riders. This one was different.

Monday morning, everyone is moving about quickly and this train slides in at a snail's pace. It sidles up to the platform provocatively, slowly surveying the people wanting it to be "their" train. All the lights were out, no trainmen were visible. It looked to me, for all intents and purposes, like a ghost train. The people on the platform shrugged and went back to their iPhones and Kindles, waiting for the ghost to leave so a real train could pull in.

More announcements, again the syllables, but then something interesting: all the lights on the "Not in Service" train flashed on in an unexpected blaze of light. The people all looked up like a row of meerkats, hopeful that this ghost had somehow returned to the living. And then, as quickly as it had come alive, it started out of the station, picking up speed as the last few cars trailed out.

And what I loved was just that the next train pulled in without any fanfare or announcement, as if nothing had happened "earlier incident"-wise and everyone boarded, with me, and we took off. I'm not sure what happened to the train, but I like to think it repeated its brief appearance at the rest of the stops on the line. A poetic flash and then gone.

A Marshmallow on the Bus

March 4 – A Girl on a Leash

In a sea of black coats, any little bit of color will attract your attention. It was icy cold this morning and everyone on the first platform, waiting for the express train, was swathed up to their ears. Black coats, gray scarves, dark hats, black gloves, and bags of every conceivable description. They too were all black or shades of black.

The train this morning was crowded, keeping everyone alert not to intrude on the space of the guy standing next to you. I looked down and saw black sneakers, black boots, black shoes. There was a man who entered the car somewhere along Central Park West carrying a paper coffee cup decorated with the iconic blue Greek temple but other than that, until we reached Queens, not another spot of color.

I wasn't paying too much attention until an older woman got on with a child. This was the first child I had seen this morning. She was walking, holding the hand of the older woman who was, in turn, holding in her other hand, the end of the girl's bright yellow leash. The girl, maybe 2, maybe 3 years old, it was hard to tell, was wearing what looked from the back to be a cute yellow backpack. But the front was lashed like a mass market version of a lifejacket and extending from the straps was a leash.

The woman sat down and lifted the girl onto her lap, never letting go of the end of the tether. The girl looked, all of a sudden, like she was part of a circus act, like a ventriloquist's dummy about to start mouthing words spoken under the breath of the older woman. She looked healthy, she looked happy, and all the while the woman tugged at the bottom of the girl's pant legs or fussed with her shoelaces, and the girl looked calmly into the car and out the windows as stations passed.

All I could think of was the time my son stepped down off a bus on 86th Street and Columbus Avenue, years ago, and then ran full out in front of the bus – and how I wanted him to be on a leash. But here's the thing about leashing a child: they never learn not to leave your side. The leash gives both the child and the guardian a false sense of security and allows the child to step away the full length of the leash – up to 5 or 6 feet away from you – instead of holding your hand, close by your side. When you unleash the child, what have they learned other than how similar they must have looked to dogs?

I never bought a leash. In no instance would I not want to hold my son's hand.

March 5 – Pardon the Interruptions

I've written many times about how same the morning rush hour is, how everyone wears black, how similarly quiet or noisy it is. Today, I looked for the anomalies, the personality, the distractions.

This is a short list of this morning's interruptions:
- 145th Street

Enter a tall, handsome dad with a little girl, about 8 or 9 years old. Dads tend not to bring children on this train. Sometimes they do, but typically this is not a train that attracts anyone with their children. There were two seats, but not together so she sat just opposite him until enough riders got off at their stops and they could sit together. What was remarkable about this? It was the moment the girl finally was able to sit down next to her dad, quickly nestling in against his arm. It was as if she had been cast adrift and then pulled into shore.

- 86th Street/CPW

I heard a gypsy violinist, playing for all he was worth. I assume it was "he" not by the character of the playing, but because I have seen a male violinist here in the past. It was frantic, wonderful, plaintive.

- Rock Center

Waiting on the platform was a tall blond woman in very skinny jeans wearing a full length fake fur coat in a leopard pattern. It was an eye-opener. It had a hood too. All leopard. Imagine.

Across the platform on the downtown side of this station, there was a man wearing a hooded sweatshirt who was standing – next to many places to sit – standing, waiting. He had two granny carts' worth of bottles and cans and he looked like anyone on their way to the supermarket to get the bottle deposit returns. Each can, each bottle will net you a few cents and it does add up. What was unusual? Other than the fact that he was standing when most people would sit, he stood there and watched as train after train came in and left, never boarding the train.

It wasn't clear to me why he would be there during rush hour, waiting for a train surrounded by his collection of bottles and cans. And since all the trains available on that platform had already come and gone, it wasn't clear what he was waiting for either.

March 6 – Out of the Frying Pan

One more morning commute on the NYC subways and I have come to realize why the quiet interests me. You stand on the platform – quietly. Games on your phone – again, quiet. Reading a Kindle or one of the free papers and it's all quiet. Other than the sound of the train car wheels on the tracks and the brakes or the singsong of the closing door signals – it's just quiet. Few conversations and even fewer distractions.

Until the train pulls into the station. Suddenly, there is a flurry of activity that did not seem possible before. It's as if a still photo were animated just by the fact that the train doors have opened. People push their way out onto the platform and into the stairs and everything is as if thrown into a giant blender, all kinds of images swirling around and together to be poured finally into the station concourse.

It's on the concourse, at the morning breakfast places, that the most dramatic shift occurs because the very same people who were silent a moment ago are now shouting out their coffee order, grabbing up bananas and donut holes off the counter, shifting their weight impatiently waiting for their order. The difference is that a moment ago, the MTA controlled their fate: once they were on the train, there was nothing in their power to move their journey forward. But now, in the light of the overhead fluorescence, their lives have been handed back to them and they make all the decisions.

And my, the grand heights of this new-found freedom to choose the next step in their lives: "Large coffee, milk, no sugar, please!" And then, they are out and on their way to work.

March 8 – Lego Movie Lego Movie

On any given day, riding either the bus or the trains in New York, I pretty much never see anyone I know. It's a big world out there. I know lots of people, having lived in New York for 35 years but I just don't see you unless we make plans to meet or I go somewhere you are already.

So, how is it I see the same guy selling DVDs and plastic toys nearly every day on the train? How could he possibly be on every train I take?

My daughter insists it's not the same guy, just a guy who might be his cousin or his brother. Whether there are many instances of him, instead of the single version I claim to be watching, or not, he comes into the train car, rattling this lightweight plastic toy to get everyone's attention. This weekend, he was selling illegal copies of the Lego movie, "Lego movie Lego movie Lego movie." The drone is unmistakable.

But I can go for an entire month not seeing anyone I know and yet I will see this guy almost every time I take the train after, say, noon. He must walk the entire length of this train line, back to front, front to back, over and over again, balancing, dipping, teetering, but never falling. The sheer physicality of his selling technique is remarkable.

I only see him sell, maybe, I don't know, a half dozen sales in a month's worth of selling? I'm sure it's more profitable than that or he'd give it up for some more legal occupation. Still, I used to think he could be selling empty cases, but not with seeing the same people over and over the way he does. If I were to buy an empty box, I would be assured he'd be on my train later and I could have it out with him.

Underground economy - more checks and balances than you might think.

March 11 – That Red Sox Guy

I was about to settle into reading my new book. It's a prize winner and the writing is captivating, but a man entered the train at Columbus Circle and I never got back to my book.

Not tall, not slim, he looked like he might have been running late. He stood out, in a sea of New Yorkers, because he was wearing a baseball cap. Oh, not just any baseball cap, mind you, a Red Sox baseball cap. He stepped into a Yankee stronghold with the arch rival's team logo on his hat. Most people never saw it, of course, because everyone had their head down, reading their Kindles, playing games on their phones.

Something was wrong with Red Sox guy though. From the moment he came on the train, he started muttering under his breath. I heard "damn" and "no" and "really?" He was wearing a red button front shirt and a red tie, decorated with large musical notes. And some kind of hang tag ID badge in a plastic holder, hanging around his neck.

He was not happy and soon became more and more agitated. He unbuttoned his tan overcoat further, down to his waist. While holding the center pole in the car, he reached into his coat with his left hand and started pulling string. It was just a 6 or 8 inch length to start, three strands together of yellow, red, and blue, but as he pulled, he became more upset, more determined, and more agitated.

The string was coming out of his coat in handfuls now as he pulled and bundled and pulled more and bundled more until he had a fistful of multi-colored string in the palm of his hand. Whatever he was unraveling started to take on the appearance of a clown in the circus or the magician who pulls scarf after connected scarf from his sleeve or his pocket.

I never got to see what was left of whatever he was unraveling, but I imagined that he too would unravel and all that would be left, on the train car floor or the edge of a platform someplace, would be a pile of unraveled him. All gone, leaving only that irritating Red Sox cap.

March 12 – Headphones

Weather watching is a very different activity if you travel underground instead of by car. When I was growing up, I do not remember ever owning an umbrella. We'd get in the car in the garage, open the door, and drive out. When we got where we were going, we'd get out at the place and I do not remember getting wet. Now, to be honest, I must have walked to school in the rain when I was a kid, but for some reason, I only remember walking in the snow.

Most folks today were in stages of weather denial, I think. I saw very little rain gear even though the forecast was for "developing" storms later in the day. It's too cold for raincoats still and most snow-friendly coats are not waterproof, so it leaves you with a random collection of apparel, not much of which really does the job. Some folks looked prepared though, carrying neatly folded tall umbrellas that they carried like walking sticks.

It was more the headphones I noticed this morning. There's something about a developing storm that causes people to close up a bit and it seemed like everyone had headphones this morning. There were the standard Candy

Crush players, of course, and a woman reading the free paper, but nearly everyone else had their headphones on.

Red headphones, black, white with the signature Apple look about them – all were in evidence. What's fun is the random buzz that spills over when you sit near someone whose headphones like to share what's on their playlist. I listened to Rihanna, and Beyoncé, some of the Pharrel Williams "Happy" song, and saw lots of head bopping to go along.

And it was like watching insulation. Each listener was insulated not only from the weather reports but from each other. Padding over the ears becomes padding all over. The only remnant? That spillover. I watched Rihanna get off at Columbus Circle, Beyoncé stayed on til 57th Street. And I left Pharrel, still happy, when I got off at Rockefeller Center. It was just like he said, a room without a roof.

March 13 – The OK Corral

One of the most common sights on New York City subways and buses is the free newspapers. There are great neighborhood papers, like the Manhattan Times, and some of the Upper West Side papers are good, but the most common – the most distributed – are the *AM New York* and the *New York Metro*. One is good, the other, not so, but most people grab them both to make sure they don't miss anything on their way downtown.

A very high percentage of this group of double newspaper grabbers will deposit their used, read paper either on the bench or on the train. The assumption is that the next guy will not have grabbed his own copies and will be just thrilled to read something cast off by the last complete stranger to sit there. The only problem is this: everyone in New York knows that something cast off by anyone, including your grandmother, is covered in Cooties.

This morning it was mad windy out. The temperature dropped overnight and the forecast was for 50 mile an hour gusts. I kept my head down as I entered the train station this morning, but these little free papers, they tend not to be able to keep their heads down. There were papers everywhere. I spotted them along the sidewalk, on the floor of the train car, left on the bench in numbers much higher than normal.

But this is New York and, where there is routine, there is frequently also a bit of magic. Since the wind was indeed gusting to double digit miles per hour, these cast off sheets of lightweight paper swirled and tumbled like tumbleweeds down the platform as the train picked up speed on its way to the next stop. I had visions of Tombstone and the Wild West, abandoned mining towns, OK Corral, Miss Kitty. The train would pass, the papers would lift and flutter, resting farther and farther down the platform.

From a forensic point of view, it would be hard to say where they started out, almost as if they were far more animated than a newspaper could possibly ever be. From my point of view though, I spent a brief moment in the Gold Rush this morning. A little something to go along with my own copy of the *AM New York*.

March 14 – The Same Page in the Hymnal

All those people and all those headphones.

I would guess that roughly 20 to 25% of morning commuters have something piped into their ears through a vast array of headphones, ranging from the free ones that come with your phone to the really expensive noise-canceling ones with the fancy colors and trademark names. I love watching how people react to all that music, whether it's just bopping to the music in their own head or inching away in disgust when their neighbor is listening to too-loud Britney Spears.

This morning, I wondered what it would be like if, at the same moment, we all took off the headphones and let the music play through the speakers. How many of us were listening to the same song, the same singer?

A Marshmallow on the Bus

I know the woman across from me had Mexican pop music. The guy next to her was mouthing along to some offensive, adult lyric rapper. And I had Katy Perry. But imagine how fabulous it would be if – just for a few minutes – we all set down our books and our bags and started to dance. Now, I am no dancer, but sometimes, I stand on that platform listening to the top 40 tunes they play on the VH-1 countdown and I want to dance. I pretend I know how.

I exited the station this morning and my personal soundtrack had moved on from Katy to Bruno Mars to Lady Gaga. It was a good morning, riding with such talent. I can't do noise-canceling headphones because I think New Yorkers really need to be able to listen to the street sounds to stay safe, but I could still tune out the traffic noise while I bopped down the street on my way to Subway to get my Veggie Delite for lunch today.

As Lady Gaga would say, "Applause, applause, applause. I live for the applause, 'plause."

March 17 – New Balance

One of the most important things you need to know to ride the New York subway system, or any other metro, is this: you have to make sure you are physically safe at all times and you have to put some thought into it. You don't wait at the very edge of the platform, you mind the gap between the train and the platform edge as you board or leave the train, you never even think about going down to the train tracks to retrieve something that's fallen, and if you don't get a seat and have to stand, you hold onto something while the train is moving.

There was a young woman this morning on the downtown B who defied that last warning. Nothing dire happened to her. She managed to keep reading her iPhone, hold a conversation with the young man standing next to her, and look all perky at the same time. But I am curious to know why she would stand within a foot of the pole in the center of this section of our train and not hold onto it?

1) She was oblivious. That's always a possibility in New York, as I suppose it is in most big cities. Sometime you just don't see things that are looking you in the face. Life can be a blur sometimes.

2) She's a germaphobe. I have a friend who once got a paper cut while she was in her office. She left for the day and grabbed that pole on the train on her way home with her paper-cut hand and ended up in the hospital, fighting a blood infection.

3) It was a test. She wanted to see if anyone noticed? The only prize would have been her ability to make a face indicating she was cooler than us.

4) She was trying to impress the young man? No. He was holding on.

As the train made its way downtown, she wobbled, she tottered, and she nearly made it all the way to Rockefeller Center unscathed. But she couldn't navigate the turns after Columbus Circle. That's when her arms went out to her sides, she got a panicky look, she nearly dropped her iPhone, and then she righted herself like a ship listing in choppy waters finally finding its balance.

She never fell and she didn't knock anyone over. But then, she was wearing New Balance sneakers – and I'm thinking, maybe I give them a try. It could be they have magical powers.

A Marshmallow on the Bus

March 18 – Paper or Plastic?

Why on earth do we carry so much stuff?

Lately, I've been watching the bags on the trains, on the platforms, on the stairs. Women carry shoulder bags and shopping bags, most men have backpacks, briefcases, or messenger bags. It's interesting to watch when one gender adopts the bag styles of another because what usually follows is something fun. People who know which bag to carry are unobtrusive, nearly invisible. But people who carry bags against type? There's something else going on there.

This morning, a fat, fat man was waiting to board the train I was on. I would never have noticed him because, sadly, fat, fat men in New York are common enough. But he was carrying a large, stuffed, rosy pink, shopping bag. This was a commuter train and most commuters – even women – won't carry such a loud color to work in the morning.

He stuffed himself onto the train and it looked like he was just going to blend into the crowd near the door when out of the blue, he shouted to everyone around him, "If everyone would just move six inches to their right, we could save a lot of time here." And so they did. Move, that is. A calculated and precise six inches to their right so he could feel more comfortable in his place by the door.

But that wasn't enough, which made me wonder how he selected six instead of eighteen for the number of inches he needed to feel at home in his new environment – my train car.

He pushed his way, holding that pink bag out in front of him, shoving into the clutch of folks already in the middle of the car, his messenger bag, the more appropriate choice for a male commuter, swinging out against the backs and sides of everyone he passed on his way to the center of the car. He then announced at full voice, "I am getting off at the next stop."

And he did. He reversed the pushing and the maneuvering so he could re-take his place near the door and then exit just as the door opened.

But it was that pink bag, and after he left, climbing the stairs out of the station at 7th Avenue, I wondered where he was going and if the rest of his day would afford him the space he needed.

March 19 – It Takes a Village

It takes a village to raise a child, but this morning, I realized sometimes it takes a village just to get through rush hour.

I got a seat this morning next to a woman who was reading the paper. I started reading my book. It's a winner and even though it's a really large book, it's worth carrying an extra canvas shoulder bag so I can read it on the train. I noticed the couple next to me on the other side, even though the train was particularly crowded due to some "activity" earlier. He looked like a jazz bass player and the woman next to him kept laying her head against his shoulder. They were a couple.

She sneezed. No one said anything. She sneezed again and the woman standing next to him offered a "God bless you." I went back to my book.

But then she started sneezing the way people do in an allergy attack. One sneeze, then "achoo achoo ahhhchoo ahchooo!" We all looked at her and she apologized. The woman sitting next to me said, "Oh no, it's alright." I offered her tissues and the woman standing next to Jazz Guy told her, "Oregano. Get the tablets. It'll knock it right out."

I got off at the next stop and went to collect my French Vanilla Latte Regular Milk No Sugar. There is a weird protocol at this particular coffee place where you order in one window and then line up at another to get your order. I ordered at Window #3 and dropped my change in my bag and headed over to Window #2 to get my drink. While I was

89

standing there, I heard someone shout and then something
falling. I thought maybe someone had dropped a full cup of
coffee on the floor, splashing it against the pants leg of some
Suit. The Suits frequent this place now.

When I looked over to the window I had just left, I
saw a 40-something woman, dressed in a business suit and
coat, sitting on the floor, pressing at her forehead as if she
had just hit her head hard against something. One of the Suits
knelt next to her and supported her upper back and the man
standing in front looked out at all of us watching as if by
some telepathy he could summon help for her.

Two rookie cops came up, two employees ran over,
the two Suits stayed with her. When I left, I felt both helpless
that I really couldn't do anything but watch, and gratified that
my fellow coffee patrons were able to help her out.

It does take a village.

March 20 – Seize the Spring!

You'd think New Yorkers would have been out
dancing in the streets today, being as it's the first day of
spring. I didn't see anything celebratory, especially not at 8:00
a.m. this morning when I was getting on my train. I suppose
it's just that we are pretty skeptical as a group. Basically, I
believe spring when I see it.

So, what is there to look for to affirm the advent of
spring in the absence of dancing or the little lame balloon
man whistling far and wee à la e.e. cummings? Other people
look for robins, but it's not every day you notice birds here,
so that's probably not a good one. Some places notice crocus
or daffodils and we get that too. But I don't plant things
outdoors so I would have to rely on somebody else to
provide these items. If I see flowers, that's all good and there
are days when I look for them. I just don't grow them myself.

On my way out this morning, I conferred with my
daughter – do we wear the lightweight jacket and run the risk
of freezing or do we bundle up and run the risk of looking

like a fashion flop? We opted for light and it was great. I felt light, I looked light, and I knew I was what you could call fashion forward, even though we all know it's really just last year's jacket.

But today, it wasn't weight, but style that alerted me that something was in the air. It was hoodies. More than the usual number of hoodies, I might add. Where folks wore hoodies under their coat last week when it was winter, today, they just wore the hoodies. It was better than light or lightweight, it was liberating. The hoodie hid and now it could come out into the open. And a practical solution it was as well, because when the sun goes down and it's back in the 40s tonight, you can just pull that hood over your head and be snugly warm enough to get from the train to your apartment.

I remember spring coats when I was a kid. You got one for Easter and you wore it when it wasn't going to rain. Rain meant you'd wear a raincoat. But the hoodie is way better than that because you still needed a raincoat and an umbrella, but with a hoodie, you just need an umbrella and *voilà!* You've got both spring coat and raincoat in one – plus that umbrella.

Hoodies is the harbinger today. Well, hoodies and somebody else's crocus. It's all fabulous. It's spring!

A Whimper

Tomorrow, I can learn how to fly,
    Today I will run, I will cook, I will clean so
    Tomorrow I can learn how to fly.

Tomorrow, I will look at the moon.
    Today I will save, I will sort, I'll make lists so
    Tomorrow I can look at the moon.

Tomorrow I will sit in a church.
    Today I will pray, I will kneel, I will stay so
    Tomorrow I can sit in a church.

Tomorrow I will go on a trip
    Today I will call, I will pack, I will plan so
    Tomorrow I can go on a trip.

Tomorrow I will love you at last.
    Today I will rest, I will pause, I will breathe so
    Tomorrow I can love you at last.

Next month the world just might end
Next month the world just might end
So today I'll buy notebooks, or pencils, or pens
Just in case next month's The End.

But if tomorrow is not to be
I will not have run or taken a trip
    Or learned how to fly,
    Or looked at the moon,
    Or prayed in a church,
    Or sat long by the sea,

Or loved you,
Or loved you, or loved you.

Ghosts and the Light

Years ago, I read in the paper that there was a term for the spectral impressions of 19th century houses and shops that are revealed when buildings are demolished in New York. They're called "ghosts." Living in a city that is under perpetual construction of one kind or another, we live with these ghosts that appear for a short while and then are buried again by the new buildings that go up in the place of the ones that come down. Some ghosts stay – they're just outlines mostly – when buildings are replaced by parking lots or parks, but for the most part, they are laid bare for only a short time and then they vanish.

I am fascinated by these ghosts. When I walk around New York, I pay little attention to buildings above street level. I'm usually in a hurry, like most New Yorkers, and I tend not to look up much, I tend not to notice much until I pass a construction site. That's when I stop to look for ghosts. This is where you can see the shadows of the old New York, the faded, older sister of modern Manhattan, in the traces of chimneys, walls, staircases, even paint and wallpaper of the older buildings that were etched into the remaining walls.

Most people think that ghosts are the remnants of human souls that can't find their way out of this life, but these architectural ghosts are different. They are the remnants of city people who lit gas lamps and bought ice from carts and whose children played in the streets. These ghosts remained after their humans left and they haunt me.

My mother always said she wanted to be an archaeologist. I think about her when I see these outlines and traces and I get a sense of the kind of place she must have known growing up in Chicago in the 1920s. There must have been a better sense of community or neighborhood than now, watching children play in the street. You can't do that in New York very much now because of the traffic and congestion, so families take kids to big playgrounds. I bet people knew everyone in the building then, because even though the apartments were bigger, the buildings themselves were smaller. I had a friend years ago who lived in the basement of a brownstone and he knew everyone in the building, but I moved last year from a large apartment building where I had lived for 13 years and we could not name more than two families.

In lots of cases, these ghosts include the outlines of bedrooms and attics and parlors where families lived and died and cared for one another in a way that we do not see in New York as much today. This is a kind of urban archaeology where you can get a sense of the past not by what's been left to us, like pots and shards, but by what's gone. What is so interesting to me is that for the time it takes me to pass by on my bus, I find myself imagining the past, trying to see the clothes, the hats, the gloves of the ladies who stepped out of the buildings on their way to shops that were probably in the exact spot where I am now. I think about how many of these New Yorkers lived in small, terrible, dark places that are gone, installed with sheetrock and fume-free paint instead of flowered wallpaper. It might not be better to live in the 21st century building that takes the place of the 19th century one that was torn down, but it is certainly different when you replace wood and plaster with reflective metals and glass.

An old white Beaux Arts building was torn down across the street from Lincoln Center, just a few years ago. As it came down, the painted image of an old advertisement was slowly revealed on one of the walls of the building just behind it. A dapper man with a walking stick appeared and was visible for a very short while – and then the new building went up and he disappeared.

In time, as the new building rises, these ghosts will all vanish and the glimpse of the past that they offer will go with them. What is comforting to me is that just down the block, someone new has just signed a contract, someone has just approved a new plan, someone has just finished a fresh draft for a brand new building that will house new families and be the home for the next generation of New Yorkers, because as charming as these old buildings can be, they were not built to last and, over time, many of them will have to go. I could say that breaks my heart, to see the sweet four and five story tenement buildings go, but I'd be lying. I love to watch new structures take their place.

Still, I am always on the lookout for the ghosts. I like to think that once the new building is up and lit with the lives of the new families who move in, that the ghosts of the building that's gone can find rest.

Becoming a Little Old Lady

My mother identified "Little Old Lady" for me as a sub group in society when I was very young. She shunned the cafe at the Marshall Field store in Chicago because she called it a "Little Old Lady Tearoom." She pointed out the various characteristics of Little Old Ladydom to me such that I always knew one when I saw one and I was armed and ready to confront whatever special little old things they might try to foist off on me, God forbid. Even though she lived to be 92, she never became a Little Old Lady. She was such a powerful force in our lives, for better or worse, that I could never relegate her to this sub group. I think that's why it fascinates me so.

As an urban anthropologist, not professionally of course, but by avocation, I like to watch people. I watch what they wear, I watch what they eat, I watch what they throw on the ground. Apparently, not everyone does this. A friend of mine used to ask me why I was so interested in people I didn't know and I never had a really solid answer other than that I enjoyed it. I don't read the tabloids or *People* or any of the paparazzi magazines, but I do find watching real live people to be quite entertaining sometimes; sometimes sad, and sometimes, more and more lately if I am forced to be honest, I find myself asking just what kind of Little Old Lady am *I* becoming.

There's the little old lady in church. She walks with a noisy cane that almost demands you watch her walk up the aisle. When I see her, I wonder what the first day with a cane must be like. How is it to go from completely independent walking to needing and using a cane which is such a symbol of old, older, infirm, dependent? How do you know that tomorrow you need a cane, but today you do not? I wonder if she was embarrassed, walking into a cane store and asking for one in her 4' 10" size. I wonder if she used it right then and there to get home. Or maybe her son gave it to her, thinking it was a nice gift, not realizing that some small bit of her was lost now.

I was in Madrid not long ago, walking along the Gran Via with my daughter, when we saw a little old man just ahead of us. The Gran Via is pockmarked with the traces and shadows of the Spanish Civil War bombings and shootings and even though it's full of fun shops and touristy restaurants now, if you look hard enough, you can see indentations of cannon balls and bits of stone that are missing. This little old man stopped and reached his hand out to caress the stone in just one of those indentations you would miss if you didn't know why they were there. He leaned forward, pressing into the stone facade of this building and covering his eyes with the other hand. That movement went through me like electricity. I felt immediately what he was doing, why he was there and I wondered if it was his father, grandfather, uncles who died. Were they saved at that spot, had he gotten the chance to say goodbye to them? Or was it a legend, passed down to the children that on that very spot, surrounded now by restaurants, something terrible happened. I think about him whenever I see photos of the Gran Via now and I wonder if he tells people about the war, what it was like in Madrid in the 1930s.

There was a marvelous little old lady in the subway station at 149th Street in the Bronx when I first moved to my new apartment. I would see her, fixed on her spot, every Sunday on my way to church and even though she was dressed in what is usually called a Church Suit, she wasn't in church and for all I could tell, wasn't going there either. She wore hats, I remember that. And gloves. You don't see that much anymore. And she handed out little folded pieces of paper that had short sermons on them. She looked perfectly in place there, standing near the stairs to the basement train level and she didn't say very much, other than to return my "Good morning," until one Sunday, when I came onto the platform and she was singing. Subway platforms, as you may not know, are acoustically vibrant places because they have little to absorb the sound. Her voice carried beautifully. I walked right up to her but instead of the usual greeting, I started to sing with her. She and I sang two verses and choruses of *Blessed Assurance* together before I accepted her flier and walked downstairs to catch my train. I have not seen her since.

Not being able to predict the future, I am not sure what will happen and I think that's what makes a lot of people anxious. I would like to have a nice cane and not a rattly one. I would like for someone to comfort me if they see me touch a stone someplace that moves me to tears and I would hope that you all will sing with me if for some reason I am moved to sing hymns on a Sunday morning in the Bronx. Becoming a bona fide Little Old Lady will take time, I think. But I like to think that I will do it, and my current favorite little old ladies – and men – proud.

Steal Me: A Very Short Poem

Steal me away to the bridge near the water,
  tall white still-standing, far-waiting for me.

Steal me away to a seat in the café,
  watching a waiter pour mint tea at arm's length.

Steal me away, far from home and from here,
  let me know the soft voice of the sea.

Steal me away so I breathe again, softly,
  Steal me so I can find strength.

The Bus to Work: A Limited Lament

In New York, there are many types of buses. Typically, the main routes have buses that stop every two blocks or so, but on weekdays, the same route offers "limited" buses that stop every ten blocks or so. They are meant, clearly, to get you to work really fast, almost before you can change your mind and call in sick. They zoom past the pokey regular buses and they are my favorites. Less so because they get me to work faster, more so because of the tiny dramas they provoke en route.

This morning, I hopped on my limited bus and saw a friend who was reading near the back. She lives farther uptown and I see her every once in a while. I brought my book today so I sat just behind her, not wanting to bother her reading and wanting to open my book. But I found myself watching the frantic people at the regular bus stops attempt to flag down my limited bus in vain. This is one of my favorites, one of the great perks of riding a limited, or express bus, if you will pardon the *schadenfreude*. You get to watch your hopelessly clueless fellow New Yorkers try to catch the attention of a bus driver on a New York City limited bus.

This particular ride offered a lone, older lady first. She was sitting on a bench, waiting patiently at a regular – not a limited – stop. The benches are fairly new and they are very convenient, especially if you have bags or packages. She caught sight of my bus, took a moment to stand, and then proceeded to wave her cane, in a decidedly threatening, mildly violent manner, at the driver of my bus. Her mouth formed words that would likely have been bleeped on television, and her face contorted in the most unfortunate way, all the while waving the cane out ahead of her as if she were standing backstage at a bad vaudeville show, getting ready to "hook" the performer. Not pretty. I wanted to paper-airplane a note to her out the window of the bus: "Please take your seat, ma'am. This bus doesn't stop here," but this scene will be resolved when the next regular bus stops, she complains to the driver while paying her fare, and the driver sets her straight.

Then there are the passengers who were, by coincidence, waiting at a limited stop and who unwittingly board the limited bus, thinking it will make all the local stops. These folks are tremendously entertaining. They ring the bell, gather their little belongings together, look around, and then watch out the window as their stop passes by. Then they shout at the driver frantically from their seat, "Hey, that's my stop, hey, you didn't pull over, hey, wait, you missed my stop!" And the driver usually just shouts back, "Limited stops!" which means, "Limited, get over yourself, I am not stopping here." Then they drag everything up to the driver, look him in the face, and start the limited lament. "You never said it was a limited, now what am I supposed to do?" And, by this time, the driver has not said anything but "Limited stops" and the bus has reached its next limited stop, usually about six blocks from the stop they wanted. They sludge off, mumbling to themselves, as the rest of us sigh collectively and go back to our books and Kindles.

This same scene plays out frequently in Spanish too, when the new passenger only knows which stop to get off and is not fluent enough in English to catch the word "Limited" even if the driver announces it. They also shout, in Spanish, from their seat, but unlike the English-speaking passengers, everyone on the bus tries to help by shouting right back at them, "*Limitado, señora, limitado!*" This will bring on a multi-passenger open discussion of the way limited buses work in New York and it's usually a mix of bad but helpful Spanish from the *gringos* on the bus and really fast Dominican Spanish from everyone else. Most days, the driver jumps in to shout back at everyone that this is indeed a limited bus. "*Limitado, señora, limitado!*"

On one hand, I wish the word "Limited" were better displayed to the bus riders waiting at non-limited stops. This way, they would know to just let it go. They were at the wrong place at the wrong time and another bus, the local that makes all the stops, will be arriving shortly. I wish the drivers, especially the ones going through Spanish-speaking neighborhoods, would make an effort to alert passengers when they board that this bus will not be making all stops. But deep down, I am enjoying the dramas. These little scenes, vignettes if you will, are what make bus riding in New York during rush hour very entertaining. Call it *schadenfreude*, call it boredom, it's lots of fun.

My book-reading friend and I can exchange a knowing glance when these lamentations begin because we've been there, we've done that ourselves. And when these folks get off and start their walk back to the stop they missed, she and I can smile because we know it's only a few blocks before someone else leaps out of their seat and shouts, "Hey, you missed my stop!"

The only real difference is that we've crossed over. It's that smug feeling New Yorkers get when we've taken just one more tiny hill in our daily battle, getting from place to place on a city bus in a teeming metropolis. We never win the war really, but every once in a while, we do take the hill.

Prayer Beads on the Train

I thought I'd catch up on my book on my way into Manhattan this morning. It's a wonderful story about an Indian researcher working in a Muslim community where everyone questions his faith. The train was a local and I'd have about 20 minutes before my stop.

The people on the train were not a distraction, but the long string of beads being turned over and over in the hands of a man opposite me pulled me away in a way I could not have anticipated. Dozens of beads were strung in a loop like a long necklace; warm, medium brown wood beads, varnished so they would slip easily over his fingers. There were short red tassels and small silver beads that marked them into thirds. His hands were moving while his thoughts were fixed on the beads.

This would not have been an event today if it hadn't been for the group of friends sitting on my return train home later in the day. There was, in my one subway car, a group of people fingering their beads, just like the ones from this morning; two middle-aged women, sitting in two different sections of the car, accompanied by one young man, and two young women. They were speaking to each other over the noise of the train and I got the impression they were visiting New York as a group. And they were all holding nearly identical prayer beads.

What struck me was how easily they all displayed their prayers in public. These beads were significantly larger than the typical worry beads I have seen before, the ones that resemble a bracelet. You know, I can't remember the last time I saw anyone using a rosary on public transportation. Rosaries are so traditional, so old fashioned, you rarely see them in use even in churches in New York, much less on the street. Yet, these subway riders were all using their beads on the train.

One woman held them between her two hands, moving the beads slowly from one hand to the other. The young man was talking the whole time, holding the beads in one hand, then absent-mindedly passing them to the other hand. The woman sitting directly opposite me held them on her lap, behind her bag, only pulling them out to move them from one section to the other, and the woman sitting just a couple of seats from me sat with her eyes closed, the beads barely moving, her prayers wrapped in her silence.

At the end of our ride, my daughter and I got off the train where we were met with the sound of a youth choir. It was Sunday, after all, and the most appropriate time for this sort of God-fearing behavior. It was a group of young adults singing in harmony in a subway station in the Bronx. The girls wore skirts that fell demurely below the knee and small white caps that kept their hair in place and the boys all had their shirts tucked into their pants. There is a Mennonite congregation that places this choir in this subway stop on Sundays in an earnest attempt at evangelization. They were passing out a CD of their hymns.

What do these two groups have in common? They share an ability to own up to their faith in a secular world. They pray and they sing their belief in their God and they do it out loud. There was no attempt to conceal the prayer beads in their pockets or to give thought to their prayers without them. The subway riders were not trying to make disciples. They were just displaying their faith and even though the choir wanted us all to know what a friend we have in Jesus, they were not at all afraid or self-conscious.

When I got home, all I could think about was my mother's wake two years ago. The priest came to say the rosary at the funeral home and I didn't have beads. I felt inadequate, like I'd missed the memo to bring rosary beads to the funeral home. I should have had beads with me, but when my mother died and I had to catch a plane in just a few hours to go home, I never thought to bring them. I could have used them in the airport, on the plane, when all I could think about was how unprepared I was for all the events to come: the funeral home, the funeral Mass, the cemetery, the family. I could have used them to focus my thoughts and to pull myself together, but I've never been a rosary out-in-the-open kind of Catholic. I've sung Christmas carols outdoors, but that's a far cry from passing out hymn CDs in a train station.

I listened to a couple of tracks on the Mennonite CD. It's a sweet, naïve, high school sound and the texts are sincere and clear. I thought about the prayer beads too, the way they all could carry them onto the train and use them in the open. So, I'm going to try carrying a rosary in my bag. I might not be ready to pull them out on the bus, my beads, but it might be good to have them.

Our Tree

"That tree's got to come down," he said.
"It's too close to the house, dear."

"I know, but it's there that we met," she said.
"It's there that we slept that first night,
Snuggled close on the ground."

"We could see the water then from this spot,
        do you remember?
It's all grown over now and the shrubs are so tall
I can barely make out the river.
But I hear the running current
And the soft wind that comes up at twilight
Moves the boughs sometimes, and
I remember."

"That tree's how we picked this place.
It was our flag, our country, our banner,
Like our selves had been here years before,
Staking out this very spot for a home."

"We were so foolish then.
We thought we could do anything, didn't we?
You with the fields, me in the school."

"It was glorious to eat the food we'd raised
And the children brought me joy.
Big Fred and Sissy growing tall,
playing under the tree,
They used to say that fairies lived inside,
Do you remember?"

"My peace is to sit on this porch now,
Watching little Fred.
He tells me he knows where to look

For the fairies his father saw
Among the leaves and branches.
And his mother, sweet Molly, brings me tea."

"I can close my eyes and see this place
Clear as day and I will, I will,
I will miss our tree," she said.

> "Sleep with me, darling," he said,
> "One last time under our tree.
> The fairies will tuck us in,
> and the sound of the river
> will sing us to sleep."

He smiled.
And she sighed.

A Hot Dog and a Dance

It was really cold last week and I was on Broadway just opposite Grey's Papaya, the iconic hot dog place on the corner of 72nd Street. I didn't want to spend much time or money on lunch so I ducked in and found myself in the midst of about two dozen tourists and two other New Yorkers. Everyone was getting a dog.

It was fun to watch the out of towners order their lunch. Everyone got a dog or two but, for the most part, they bought soda to drink, missing the real glory of this place – the fresh juices. It must have been a visiting high school sports team or debating club because there was a big bus parked just outside and two older women at the head of the line were paying for everyone's lunch. They all bought and then quickly filed back on the bus.

As I got up to the front to order, I started to listen to the music on the overhead speakers. It was Whitney Houston with *I Wanna Dance with Somebody*.

Since I was still waiting in line, I was playing with my phone and without thinking, I started to sing along and dance a bit.

In front of me was a burly construction guy with a fat architect's pencil stuck behind his ear. He was dancing. And across from me, the third New Yorker, a homeless man with a hoodie, holding the door open in the hope of getting a tip, was dancing too. When the chorus came around in the music on the box, all three of us started singing together, as the last of the high school kids left with their lunch.

Now, it's just us, singing and moving a bit to the beat. The construction guy left after getting his lunch and I got my small piña colada and my hot dog with sauerkraut and stood near the windows at the front to eat my lunch. I watched the homeless man walk across and behind me.

I expected him to leave as well but he came over to me and said, "Hey, girlfriend, you better stay warm, OK?"

I offered to buy him a dog, but he graciously declined and started in on his speech, looking for a donation instead.

"I'm just out of prison," he started. "I've got some domestic problems, you know. I'm Rick and I'm 64."

I looked right at him.

"Rick, I'm going to be 62 tomorrow!" I told him, just finishing my drink and gathering up my things to leave.

"No kidding!" he responded. "Give me your phone number so I can call you and take you dancing tomorrow for your birthday!"

I smiled at him and slowed down for just a second to say, "Stay warm, Rick," and I gave him some ones.

He followed me out on the street, reminding me to stay warm, too – and to have a happy birthday.

Don't you wanna dance with somebody?

Watching

What am I doing here?
Here I am sitting in this church and
It's a Mass of Healing.
But I'm not sick, you know.

I'm not like sick, you know, like coughing
or like really sick, you know.
I keep my head down so they won't know
I'm not one of them,
You know, not sick, you know, like them,
the sick people.
I wonder what's wrong with her? With him?
What am I doing here?

Maybe she's got stress, that's it,
maybe she's got stress.
Maybe she's got something wrong
I can't see from here.
I lean forward to get a better look.
She doesn't look sick.

What am I doing here?
I'm totally fine.

There's the priest to everyone stand,
Get in line, everyone come on down
for the anointing of the sick!
How is it I am the only one not to stand?

I try to look nonchalant, you know,
like I am just sitting here.
They will know I don't belong here.
They must know I'm just watching them.
Watching.

A Marshmallow on the Bus

Oh, what could it hurt if I play along?
So what if I'm not sick and I just play along?
That's not cheating, it's just what I can do so they don't
think anything at all.
So I can just sit here,
Watching.

> I thought you'd come home by now.
> I thought you'd miss us, miss me,
> miss us.

So, I get in a line and look down and pretend
I can stand up front and be saved, be cured,
be blessed whatever.
I can totally look the part, eyes spilling tears,
I can weep at the touch of the sacred oil
to my clear head, to my empty hands.

And walking back, I wonder if you are getting
what you need,
what you wanted, so far away.

Just because you are gone, doesn't mean
I stop looking for you as I walk up our hill.

Just because you are gone, doesn't mean
I stop seeing you.
I see you in every tall slim smart handsome beautiful child

But I don't see, you.

I don't feel saved, I don't feel cured,
the sacred oil does not bless me.
My soul is heavy sick with loss
and this oil does nothing for me.

The sick walking out, smiling, blessed.

A Marshmallow on the Bus

I walking out.

I stop on our hill.
Watching.

The Little Sinkhole That Ate Manhattan

OK, who did that? Who broke up one of the cement sidewalk squares next to my bus shelter, broke it into little bits and then just walked away? I'll let you know right off the bat, I called it "In." I am a citizen and I am walking here and I reported it.

But the question remains, how do you walk down the street and smash the bejeezus out of one sidewalk square and move on? Did you drop something? Was it an "oops" moment where you were carrying a 500 pound metal ball on your shoulders and some pretty girl walked by and caught your eye? "Oops," really?

Or did the Incredible Hulk step there with his green hulk toes while bounding across Broadway?

Sure, sure, like that happened.

Maybe there was a bad guy. You know you always have to be on the look-out for bad guys. Maybe there was a bad guy and he, and he, maybe he?

OK, we can rule out bad guys. That's always a relief when you can rule out bad guys.

Fresh Direct delivery guys? They were unloading their truck and dropped one of the watermelons they were delivering to the seminary on the block. They were delivering a crate of watermelons to the seminary on the block?

OK. Not the Fresh Direct guys either.

Neighborhood kids. Isn't it always the neighborhood kids? They were skateboarding down the block and thought it'd be really cool to have a trough to jump their boards over. So they all got together and jumped up and down at once and then, "Drat, we broke the street."

I think the kids are off the hook on this one.

Mail? Could have been the mail man, setting down his really heavy mailbag so he could open that blue mailbox? Oh, I doubt it. Who sends paper mail anymore anyway?

So, I avoid the obvious. I look for the simple, human-generated answer. I want it to be bad guys, delivery guys, mail guys, or neighborhood kids. But I think it's a sink hole. I think it's the start of something big. This is the rumble on the block, the street sucking us in. The buildings will go next because the City is not going to send out their "311" team to look into a single busted square on a really big sidewalk in a teeming metropolis. This thing will grow and devour and suck us all in until there's no more seminary, or mailbox, or bus shelter. Then it's going to suck in the subway line and the #1 train line will go dark and people will be stranded and scared.

Run for your lives, fellow Morningside Heightsers! Get out while you can!

Or it could be old, poorly maintained cement with not enough support underneath. But who knows?!?!?! Arghhhhhh!

It's just a tale told by a local rabble rouser, signifying nothing.

But you gotta love the sound and fury, right?

UPDATE and POSTSCRIPT

The City has erected Orange Conehenge. We are saved. The City is fixing the sidewalk!

A Noodle Ode

On my way to work yesterday, I was stopped in my tracks, prohibited from further advance, by the sight of a lone noodle at the top of the stair landing in my building. I was in a rush, having just spilled hot coffee all over the floor in the kitchen and having spent my last few moments mopping up the mess. But the noodle wasn't going anywhere. Strategically placed in the middle of my path, it cried out to me for further examination. I opted just to keep walking, leaving it lying there, awaiting its next encounter with a human in a hurry.

But even though I left it there, I couldn't help wondering who leaves a noodle on the floor like that? Was someone sitting at the top of those stairs, eating their noodles, and one got away? How could you not see it when you packed up your plastic fork, the tin container, and your paper bag after, presumably, consuming the rest of the noodles?

So, I thought, it's interesting. Tourists come to New York from all over the world to look at the tall buildings and here I am stressing over a lonely, floor-bound noodle. I realize I am craving order these days, for some reason. I want things to fit in boxes. I want columns to add up at the bottom. I have a real need for things to be tidy, clean, neat, simple, unencumbered.

I could use a vacation. And I want to go someplace where folks pick up their damn noodles.

This particular staircase is my egress, my exit strategy. I love to take the elevator up and the stairs down because I think that gives me some exercise even though I know, deep down, it would be better in reverse. I should take the stairs up. Funny thing about this staircase though is the pitch is a little off. The angle of the stair placement is such that you feel like you are climbing a rope ladder. The treads are fine, and the height of the risers is fine, but the pitch is off enough that the stairs feel really tall. It's why I don't walk up. Sometimes, walking down is a little floopy too.

A Marshmallow on the Bus

I suppose I should have picked up the noodle. It would have been a kindness. I could have deposited it in the trash on the way out the door, but I was in a rush. It's just what you do when you are on your way out. You just walk over the noodle and keep moving.

It was gone when I got home.

My Little Boat

My little boat is ready.
I am waiting on the shore.
I have gathered up my things
and hold them close.
But what shall I take with me
when I don't know where I'm going?
What do I put inside my little boat?

I want to take my words,
I want to keep my thoughts
They are all sorted so nicely and so clean.
I won't fit all my pictures,
and I can't fit all my ghosts.
What if I don't remember where I've been?

What if I choose my favorites
and leave the rest behind?
I can't pick out among them, there's no way.
My boat is too too small,
but the sea is still my friend.
So I wait here on the shore, I wait all day.

What if I take it all and then I sail away?
Will someone know I'd been here just before?
Will I find you all tomorrow
and remember what we had?
Or will I still be standing on the shore?

Train Whistle and Then Gone

Getting ready for bed just now, I heard a train whistle out my window. It's been a little warmer, more like spring, and I've started leaving the windows open just a crack at night to get some air. This train was not all that way off in the distance, probably ten blocks or so from my apartment, but I heard that first punch of the whistle as the train comes out into the open after leaving Grand Central and the labyrinth of tunnels that take trains north into the suburbs and away, and I stopped to listen for it again.

I grew up with trains crossing fresh fields taking fruit and vegetables from the farms near my house into the city. It was exciting. We used to wave at the engineers and count the cars every time we'd stop in the car at a lowered crossing gate, watching the trains cross in front of us. But it's a very different sense you get of trains when they are transporting people instead of cargo. The same sound that used to mean that something fun was about to happen now, a game even, sounds just as lonely as it's always described. The lonely sound of the train whistle, disappearing into the lonely night, isn't that it? That sound leaves a hollow, empty echo of the trains as they dissolve in the distance with just enough of the rumbling sound of all that metal on the tracks to remind you of their size, their weight, their speed.

Traveling on trains used to be an elegant business in my family, all white gloves and bar cars. When I was little, my grandfather would take us into Chicago on the trains to go to political events and parades. We would dress up with hats and patent leather shoes and he'd introduce us to the train men as if we were celebrities. I felt so grown up.

There it is again.

The train is getting farther away now. The whistle competes with the sound of traffic, car radios, and horns.

That whistle should call up images of folks going home from work or visiting family, going out to dinner, or getting away for a few days. But it doesn't. It sounds like heartbreak and loss, as if the train is separating people instead of bringing them together. Running down the platform, waving for the trainman not to leave without you, settling into a seat, glancing out the window, but there's nobody there. The whistle is about loneliness, leaving. It never reminds me of coming together, only of coming apart.

So, how is it that the one calling card of the train displays such sad sentiment when the whole purpose of trains is to take people where they are going, and bring them closer to where they want to be? I'm going to take one of these trains in a few days that will bring me to the airport so I can fly out to visit my family. But I know already, having done this so many times, that I will feel wistful, anxious, and unsettled doing so. And I think it's that whistle. Once you start to move out of the station, you hear the whistle and it means leaving, not going. I won't be *going* to visit, I'll be *leaving* my home. Why is there no neutral ground?

It could just be that I need to take trains more often so that I can remember how thrilling it was, sitting in the back seat of the car, hearing the ding of the bells as the gate was being lowered, and waiting to catch the first sight of the engine or the last sight of the man on the platform in the caboose. When I was in high school, we'd shout out at the engineers and the trainmen to see if they would wave back to us so we could tell our friends that we'd made contact. We were stuck in place, but they were going someplace. These guys were working on the railroad, and moving freight. They stood for progress and Made in America.

There, I don't hear it now.

The passengers on that train are probably out of the city, on their way north, maybe all the way to Albany or Montreal. Should get there in a couple of hours. Just enough travel time to catch up on that book or finish that report that's due tomorrow. Maybe when they come back, they will take in a show or try a new restaurant. Maybe they are gone for good, giving up on the city and whatever brought them here.

When I am on a train, hearing that whistle, it sounds to me like, "Get out of my way, I am coming through! I've broken free of the city and the vast open stretches of American prairies and fields lay out before me."

It's nothing but empty bravado, but I love it.

Are You Retired?

Coming home from work just now, and please allow me to emphasize the word "work," I found myself crossing the street just behind a neighbor from my building. My children and I are fairly new to the building, so I know only a handful of people and next to no names but this particular woman is familiar to me because her daughter lives on my floor and I've seen them together.

"Hi, how are you?"

Drat, I hate small talk. I'm just no good at it. If I had to give myself a grade the way Suze Orman's call-in guests have to grade how well they are doing in their personal finances, I'd give me a D. Great at personal finance, lousy at small talk. I start and finish with lame, canned, scripted weather comments that run the gamut from "It sure is windy" to "Can't wait to get the fan going." You get the idea.

Today we quipped with alacrity about breezes coming in through open windows; my forgetting mine were open, she preferring sweaters and blankets to radiator heat. I managed to hold my own for roughly a minute and a half and I was feeling pretty smug about it and was close to upping my D to a C- when the proverbial rug went right out from under me as she asked: "So, do you work, or are you retired?"

What?

The expression on my face must have brought new meaning to the term deer in the headlights.

"I work. You know. No, not retired yet," smiling, awkward pause, getting the wrong keys out of my bag, fummydiddling with the lock the way really old people do with keys and locks.

In a flash, I think, "What, do I look really old?" and "Wow, I thought *you* were older than me!" and "Should I never wear this shirt again?" and "How could you say that?"

In the span of three uttered words, she made me feel like the crypt keeper. But, here's the thing. I don't think about retiring. I have a routine. I go to work and they pay me. There are days, boy, are there days, when I wish I could be anywhere else, but I tell my children, that's why they call it work. Some days, it's not a picnic. It's work. But I get vacation days so I can bug out when I need to.

To me, retiring is just getting really poor in a hurry. Retiring is admitting defeat. Retiring is what army generals do so they get to be called "Retired General So-and-so." But I work at a desk. If I retire, wouldn't I just be working at MY desk at home? And for no salary?

Call me Baby Boomer, but I am just not ready, even though my assistant asked me once, "So, do you think you are going to be a writer when you retire?" I wanted to say, "I don't even know what I want to be when I grow up, let alone when I retire!"

I know, I know what you are thinking: how could I be any good at all at personal finance and so full out lousy at retirement planning? It's kind of like that "one hand clapping" Zen thing. I can do the whole retirement plan thing when I have resolved the "sound of one hand clapping" thing first, OK? And, in the interest of full disclosure, I guess I am ready to admit I'm starting to look at possible volunteer jobs along with some properties I could see myself buying in Spain. It's cheaper than living in New York. And I do so want to be a writer.

So, just like Scarlett O'Hara in the *Gone With the Wind* movie, I promise to think about it tomorrow when I am at Tara. Or, when confronted with my neighbor again, I guess.

When I do retire, I want, at very least, not to *look* retired. I will not mind looking tired from jet lag or hiking. But looking retired, not so much.

About the Author

Anne Born is a Michigan-born, Bronx-based writer who has been writing stories and poetry since childhood. She blogs on *Open Salon* (as Nilesite) and *Red Room* (as Anne Born) and is a contributing writer at *The Broad Side.* Her writing focuses on family and life in a big city after growing up in a small one.

She is a photographer who specializes in photos of churches, cemeteries, and the Way of St. James in Spain. Most of her writing is done on a New York City bus or a subway train.

Anne is also the organizer of the NYC Family History Writing Meetup.

You can follow Anne on Twitter @nilesite or visit her website: http://thebackpackpress.com.

A Marshmallow on the Bus